# Fisher Investments
# on Materials

# FISHER INVESTMENTS PRESS

Fisher Investments Press brings the research, analysis, and market intelligence of Fisher Investments' research team, headed by CEO and *New York Times* best-selling author Ken Fisher, to all investors. The Press will cover a range of investing and market-related topics for a wide audience—from novices to enthusiasts to professionals.

### Books by Ken Fisher
*The Ten Roads to Riches*
*The Only Three Questions That Count*
*100 Minds That Made the Market*
*The Wall Street Waltz*
*Super Stocks*

### Fisher Investments Series
*Own the World*
Aaron Anderson

### Fisher Investments On Series
*Fisher Investments on Energy*
*Fisher Investments on Materials*

FISHER
INVESTMENTS
PRESS

# Fisher Investments on Materials

Fisher Investments

with

Brad W. Pyles and Andrew S. Teufel

**WILEY**

John Wiley & Sons, Inc.

Published by John Wiley & Sons, Inc., Hoboken, New Jersey.

Published simultaneously in Canada.

For general information on our other products and services or for technical support, please contact our Customer Care Department within the United States at (800) 762-2974, outside the United States at (317) 572-3993 or fax (317) 572-4002.

Wiley also publishes its books in a variety of electronic formats. Some content that appears in print may not be available in electronic books. For more information about Wiley products, visit our website at www.wiley.com.

*Library of Congress Cataloging-in-Publication Data:*

Fisher Investments.
  Fisher Investments on materials / Fisher Investments with Brad W. Pyles, Andrew S. Teufel.
     p.   cm. — (Fisher Investments Press)
  Includes bibliographical references and index.
  ISBN 978-0-470-28544-2 (pbk.)
     1. Mineral industries.   2. Chemical industries.   3. Forest products industry.
  4. Raw materials.   5. Investments.   I.   Pyles, Brad W.   II. Teufel, Andrew S.
  III.   Title.
  HD9506.A2F53   2009
  338.2—dc22

                                                      2008040636

Printed in the United States of America

10  9  8  7  6  5  4  3  2  1

# Contents

# Foreword

I'm delighted to introduce *Fisher Investments on Materials*, the next investing guide from Fisher Investments Press—the first imprint ever from a money management firm. My firm places a heavy premium on investor and client education, making us, I believe, unusual in the industry. Not only in the market education tools and opportunities we provide clients, but in the belief investor education is vital to what we do. This imprint is simply an extension of our continual efforts to advance our own and others' understanding of capital markets.

This particular series focuses on the standard economic sectors—from Energy to Consumer Staples to Industrials. We'll cover all 10, plus some regions, and other specific market categories vital to today's global investor.

Many folks think Materials, then commodities, then immediately gold, particularly since gold was hot for much of this century's first decade. Wrong! Thinking too small. Gold mining is part of Materials, but relatively not as important as you may think. This book covers the entire Materials universe—Metals & Mining (gold, of course, but also steel, aluminum, and other metals), Chemicals, Construction Materials, even Paper & Forest Products. The book provides a broad overview of the global sector's industries and sub-industries, as well as sector history. It also discusses issues unique to Materials stocks: How important are emerging markets? What about geopolitics? Should you invest directly in commodities like gold?

But it also provides a framework for understanding the sector's and its industries' drivers so anyone—novices, hobbyists, even new professionals—can begin forming their own forward-looking sector analysis. And it provides an investing methodology—part of the same one used at my firm for making investing decisions—that can be used no matter the economic or market conditions.

What you won't find here are hot stock tips. You won't get a formula or a list of instructions on what to buy when. Such things don't exist, and books purporting magic formulae are fiction. If you can just believe that, then the price of this book is worth it. Investing success only comes when you can know something others can't, and this book is intended to help you do that. And though this book focuses on Materials, the concepts and methodology presented are applicable to other sectors and the broader market, to help you toward greater investing success your entire investing career. Enjoy the book, and enjoy the journey.

Ken Fisher
CEO of Fisher Investments
Author of the *New York Times* best seller,
*The Only Three Questions That Count*

# Preface

*The Fisher Investments On* series is designed to provide individual investors, students, and aspiring investment professionals the tools necessary to understand and analyze investment opportunities, primarily for investing in global stocks.

Within the framework of a "top-down" investment method (more on that in Chapter 7), each guide is an easily accessible primer to economic sectors, regions, or other components of the global stock market. While this guide is specifically on Materials, the basic investment methodology is applicable for analyzing any global sector, regardless of the current macroeconomic environment.

Why a top-down method? Vast evidence shows high-level, or "macro," investment decisions are ultimately more important portfolio performance drivers than individual stocks. In other words, before picking stocks, investors can benefit greatly by first deciding if stocks are the best investment relative to other assets (like bonds or cash), and then choosing categories of stocks most likely to perform best on a forward-looking basis.

For example, a Technology sector stock picker in 1998 and 1999 probably saw his picks soar as investors cheered the so-called "New Economy." However, from 2000 to 2002, he probably lost his shirt. Was he just smarter in 1998 and 1999? Did his analysis turn bad somehow? Unlikely. What mattered most was stocks in general, and especially US technology stocks, did great in the late 1990s and poorly entering the new century. In other words, a top-down perspective on the broader economy was key to navigating markets—stock picking just wasn't as important.

*Fisher Investments on Materials* will help guide you in making top-down investment decisions specifically for the Materials sector. It shows how to determine better times to invest in Materials, what Materials industries and sub-industries are likelier to do best, and how individual stocks can benefit in various environments. The global Materials sector is complex, covering many sub-industries and countries, each with unique characteristics. Using our framework, you should be better equipped to identify their differences, spot opportunities, and avoid major pitfalls.

This book takes a global approach to Materials investing. Most US investors typically invest the majority of their assets in domestic securities; they forget America is less than half of the world market by weight—over 50 percent of investment opportunities are outside our borders. This is especially true in Materials. Many of the world's largest Materials firms are based in foreign nations, including several in emerging markets. Since the vast majority of the world's natural resources are located outside of the US and operated by non-US firms, it's vital to have a global perspective when investing in Materials today.

## USING YOUR MATERIALS GUIDE

This guide is designed in three parts. Part I, "Getting Started in Materials," discusses vital sector basics and Materials' high-level drivers. Here we'll discuss Materials' main drivers—basic materials prices—and provide eight simple questions to help you understand and form an opinion on any basic material. We'll also discuss additional drivers affecting the sector that ultimately drive Materials stock prices.

Part II, "Next Steps: Materials Details," walks through the next step of sector analysis. We'll take you through the global Materials sector investment universe and its diverse components. With so much focus on higher metal prices in recent years, it's easy to forget Materials isn't just about copper, gold, steel, and the other metals—though they are certainly important. There are currently 15 sub-industries within the global Materials sector. We take you through each in detail—including how they operate within the sector and what specifically drives each sub-industry—so you can analyze the current operating environment to choose which sub-industry will most likely outperform or underperform looking forward.

Part II also details where to find and how to interpret publicly available industry data to assist in your decision-making process. It's possible to get the necessary data for making educated bets on basic material prices, sub-industries, and individual stocks using just a handful of websites and publications. You'll learn how to critically look at a sector: what to look for, what resources you can use, what the challenges are.

Part III, "Thinking Like a Portfolio Manager," delves into a top-down investment methodology and individual security analysis. You'll learn to ask important questions like: What are the most important elements to consider when analyzing mining or chemical firms? What are the greatest risks and red flags? This book gives you a five-step process to help differentiate firms so you can identify ones with a greater probability of outperforming. We'll also discuss a few investment strategies to help determine when and how to overweight specific sub-industries within the sector.

Note: We've specifically kept the strategies presented here high level so you can return to the book for guidance no matter the market conditions. But we also can't possibly address every market scenario and how markets may change over time. And, many additional considerations should be taken into account when crafting a portfolio strategy, including your own investing goals, your time horizon, and other factors unique to you. Therefore, you shouldn't rely solely on the strategies and pointers addressed here, as they won't always apply. Rather, this book is intended to provide general guidance and help you begin thinking critically not only the about Materials sector, but investing in general.

Further, *Fisher Investments on Materials* won't give you a "silver bullet" for picking the right Materials stocks. The fact is the "right" Materials stocks will be different in different times and situations.

Instead, this guide provides a framework for understanding the sector and its industries so that you can be dynamic and find information the market hasn't yet priced in. There won't be any stock recommendations, target prices, or even a suggestion whether now is a good time to be invested in the Materials sector. The goal is to provide you with tools to make these decisions for yourself, now and in the future. Ultimately, our aim is to give you the framework for repeated, successful investing. Enjoy.

# Acknowledgments

Anumber of colleagues and friends deserve tremendous praise and thanks for helping make this book a reality. We would like to extend our tremendous thanks to Ken Fisher for providing the opportunity to write this book. Jeff Silk deserves our thanks for constantly challenging us to improve and presenting new and insightful questions as fast as we can answer them. Our colleagues at Fisher Investments also deserve tremendous thanks for continually sharing their wealth of knowledge, insights, and analysis. Without these people the very concept of this book would never have been possible.

We'd also like to thank Joseph Hall for turning every graph and table in this book from an idea into a reality. We owe a huge debt of gratitude to Michael Hanson and Lara Hoffmans, without whose guidance, patience, and editing contributions this book would not have been completed. We'd like to thank Dina Ezzat for her hard work, and thoroughness in editing and assistance with citations and sources. Evelyn Chea also deserves thanks for her eye for detail and editing contribution. Without Leila Amiri we would have been utterly lost in our attempts to implement graphics and images. Marc Haberman, Molly Lienesch, and Fabrizio Ornani were also instrumental in the creation of Fisher Investments Press, which created the infrastructure behind this book. Of course this book would also not be possible without our data vendors, so we owe a big thank you to Thomson Datastream, Thomson Reuters, Global Financial Data, and Standard & Poor's. We'd also like to thank our team at Wiley for their support and guidance throughout this project, especially David Pugh and Kelly O'Connor.

Brad Pyles would also like to specifically thank Theodore Gilliland for assisting with his full-time research responsibilities while he was working on this book. Most importantly, however, he would like to thank his wife Tina for her never-ending patience, tolerance, love, and support, as this book could not have been completed without it.

# Fisher Investments
# on Materials

# I

# GETTING STARTED IN MATERIALS

# 1

# MATERIALS BASICS

A house, office building, car, paved road, manufacturing plant, power plant, TV, and computer all have one thing in common: None would be possible without the use of basic materials. Unless you're living under a rock in the middle of the Amazon, you probably depend upon a variety of basic materials everyday. Modern society would not exist without them.

This book's goal is to help you gain a basic understanding of the Materials sector, its components, drivers, challenges, and history, as well as be a general guide to Materials investing success. Wherever possible, we'll also help you *think critically* about the sector to generate your own views, rather than just dictating a bunch of rules. Successfully investing in Materials companies does not require a PhD in chemistry or geology. What is important is a firm grasp of the laws of supply and demand, and understanding what drives the earnings and stock prices of Materials companies.

This chapter covers the basics of the Materials sector, including an overview of common traits across material producers, how materials are priced, and a primer on how basic materials are extracted and processed. At this point, we're just looking at the firms and their structures. In later chapters, we'll translate a firm's structure into performance (earnings, profitability, productivity, etc.) and detail how to use that to build an appropriate portfolio strategy.

## MATERIALS 101

Let's start with the basics. What's the Materials sector made of? If you said "commodities," you'd have plenty of company, but you'd be wrong. Technically, a *commodity* is anything with no differentiation in quality (i.e., it's generally *fungible*—one unit of specified size and characteristics is perfectly interchangeable with any other unit). In other words, gold is gold.

But not all commodities fall in the Materials sector. Most notably oil, by far the largest commodity of all by value, falls in the Energy sector. Most agricultural products—also commodities—are found in the Consumer Staples sector.

The Materials sector is composed largely of metals, chemicals, paper, lumber, cement, crushed rock (called construction aggregate), and packaging. As Chapter 4 will cover, these products are not equally represented in the sector—some are more important than others (i.e., they drive more revenue). But before we get into the specific industries, let's cover some broad characteristics all Materials firms generally share.

### Materials Are Extremely Capital Intensive

Perhaps the most common Materials trait is capital intensity. From multibillion dollar mines with construction lead times up to 10 years, to enormous chemical, steel, and paper plants where size and economies of scale can be vital, the sector features some of the most *capital intense* industries in the world.

It takes tremendous money to start a new business in these industries, often hundreds of millions or even billions of dollars. The nearby picture shows a large machine sometimes used in coal mining. Notice how small the white cars are in the bottom left. The Materials sector is characterized by *huge* machines, *huge* mines, and *huge* manufacturing plants—not many mom-and-pop shops in these industries. This creates a tremendous barrier to entry for new entrants and provides significant pricing power. As Chapter 4 covers in greater detail, it also creates concentrated industries dominated by a small number of large firms.

Capital investments in Materials firms are not made for next year, but for long time horizons. With the rapid pace of technological innovation and the inherent difficulty in long-term forecasting, today's business investments are often failures. This creates significant shifts in industry leadership over time with new companies with new technologies overtaking older and once-dominant firms.

Table 1.1 lists the 10 largest domestic Materials firms (including Canada) in 20-year intervals, starting in 1965. The order changes frequently with many once-dominant firms falling off the list or disappearing entirely. Three of the top six 1965 firms no longer exist today (Union Carbide, Bethlehem Steel, and Inco Ltd).

Not all firms that disappeared went bankrupt. Some were acquired by stronger competitors aiming to enhance the targets' values with updated technology or a new strategy.

**Coal Excavator at Work**
*Source:* Getty Images.

## Table 1.1    Largest US and Canadian Materials Firms

| Company | Market Cap (Million US$) |
| --- | --- |
| **1965** | |
| Du Pont (E I) De Nemours | $ 11,012 |
| Union Carbide Corp. | $ 4,137 |
| United States Steel Corp. | $ 2,829 |
| Inco LTD | $ 2,675 |
| Dow Chemical | $ 2,326 |
| Bethlehem Steel Corp. | $ 1,856 |
| Alcoa Inc. | $ 1,642 |
| International Paper | $ 1,342 |
| Weyerhaeuser Co. | $ 1,218 |
| FMC Corp. | $ 1,198 |
| **1985** | |
| Du Pont (E I) De Nemours | $ 16,333 |
| Dow Chemical | $ 7,797 |
| Union Carbide Corp. | $ 4,792 |
| Weyerhaeuser Co. | $ 3,995 |
| Allegheny Technologies Inc. | $ 3,868 |
| Gulf Canada Corp. | $ 3,412 |
| Fort Howard Corp. | $ 3,292 |
| Alcoa Inc. | $ 3,133 |
| PPG Industries Inc. | $ 3,023 |
| Alcan Inc. | $ 2,894 |
| **2005** | |
| Dow Chemical | $ 42,381 |
| Du Pont (E I) De Nemours | $ 39,083 |
| Alcoa Inc. | $ 25,734 |
| Newmont Mining Corp. | $ 23,912 |
| Monsanto Inc. | $ 17,121 |
| Praxair Inc. | $ 17,071 |
| International Paper | $ 16,482 |
| Weyerhaeuser Co. | $ 16,266 |
| Alcan Inc. | $ 15,230 |
| Barrick Gold Corp. | $ 14,994 |

Source: Standard & Poor's Compustat® Database,[1] 12/31/2007.

## Materials Are Hypersensitive to Economic Growth

Besides capital intensity, it's crucial to remember *economic growth is vital to Materials performance*. The reason can be directly related to supply and demand. In the short term, supply of any material is relatively fixed because bringing a new mine online takes a lot of time and effort. Outside of unexpected supply disruptions (natural disasters, strikes, etc.), strong or weak demand is the biggest determinant in basic material prices (and therefore firm profitability) over short periods.

Most products coming from the Materials sector have extremely long useful lives. Once installed, it takes years for steel to corrode, cement to break down, or plastic to wear out. When archeologists discovered a copper plumbing system in the Egyptian pyramid of the Pharaoh Khufu, it was still in serviceable condition 5,000 years after construction![2] Absent economic growth, particularly in the construction and manufacturing industries, demand can drop considerably and be easily outstripped by existing supply.

Pretend you're a factory owner. To increase production, you must build a new factory or expand your existing one. The construction takes metal, concrete, and so on. But if you're content to maintain production, other than occasional maintenance and steady use of any basic material in your product, you require no additional basic materials to maintain your existing production capacity. With no growth, demand for Materials doesn't just decline, it often falls precipitously. The combination of economic sensitivity and extremely high fixed-costs makes Materials firms very cyclical with large historic booms and busts. The high fixed cost structure creates significant operating leverage, which fuels tremendous profits during boom times and tremendous losses during busts, since raising or lowering production volumes only modestly changes total costs.

Though economic growth is a vital component of *demand*, you should be concerned about both supply and demand in your Materials analysis.

## Will We Ever Run Out of Metal?

No! First, most metals can be recycled without any loss in performance or quality. It's estimated around 80 percent of all copper ever produced is still in use today. More importantly, as a metal (or any good) becomes increasingly scarce relative to demand, its price will rise, providing incentive for innovation and substitution. Free markets are incredibly adaptive and innovative.

An example of substitution can be found in the copper market. As the price of copper increased over 300 percent from 2003 to 2008, copper wiring became increasingly expensive. Consumers looked for alternatives and by 2008, cheaper copper-clad aluminum wire made inroads as a substitute.

On the other hand, an example of innovation can be found in the nickel market. When nickel prices rose over 400 percent from 2003 to May of 2007, a dramatic incentive arose for stainless steel producers (who consume two-thirds of the world's nickel production) to find cheaper production methods. This led to the re-introduction and improvement of an alternative processing method deemed inefficient at lower nickel prices. The new process allowed huge deposits of low-grade nickel to be used in production. The sudden increase in supply helped nickel prices fall 50 percent from the middle of May through the end of 2007.

Reported known metal reserves also don't represent all the known metal in the world. Metal reserves simply represent the estimated amount of known metal that can be mined for a profit at a given price. The price used for calculating reserves is often well below the current price. A margin of error is prudently built in to ensure long-term profitability should prices fall. As prices rise, the level of reserves also increases as less economical mines become profitable.

Between higher prices, increased exploration, and improved extraction techniques, metal reserves are likely to grow for a long time. For example, global copper reserves increased from 90 million tons in 1950, to 280 million tons in 1970, to 480 million tons in 2006.

*Source:* European Copper Institute; Bloomberg Finance L.P.; International Copper Study Group.

## What's So Important About Supply and Demand?

The concept of supply and demand will come up a lot in this book, so let's tackle the topic head-on.

In a free market, prices are ultimately set by the interaction of supply and demand. A price is simply the representation of how scarce a good is and how much it's desired or valued.

Put another way, the global economy works on the same principle as a third-grader trading his potato chips for his friend's brownie. The value of that brownie depends on how much the third-grader wants it, how many other brownies or close substitutes are readily available, and how many competitors (schoolmates) have similar potato chips on the market. The brownie's worth or price is dependent on the interaction of the demand and available supply.

Although simple, never underestimate the power of this concept! Supply and demand determine prices for stocks, bonds, commodities, real estate, and virtually any other free market good.

## COMMODITY PRICING BASICS

With globalization and trade rapidly growing, most basic materials are priced globally. This is possible because they're non-perishable (i.e., iron ore, cement, and steel deteriorate very slowly) and fungible.

Depending on availability, regional pricing differences may exist due to shipping costs and import or export taxes (tariffs). If regional pricing differs by more than the cost of shipping and taxes, a producer has an incentive to ship goods to the higher-priced region and sell them there. This incentive typically keeps regional prices relatively in line with each other.

The lower the value-to-weight ratio and the smaller the end market, the more likely regional differences exist since shipping costs become a larger percentage of total costs. Table 1.2 outlines the various costs of some common basic materials. It's very cost effective to ship gold, which was over $800 an *ounce* at the end of 2007, but often uneconomical to ship construction aggregate, which cost less than $10 a *ton*. And if only a few tons are needed, economies of scale are lost and the shipping becomes even more uneconomical. Therefore, gold prices have less regional disparity than construction aggregate.

## Table 1.2  Basic Material Price Comparison

| Material | Price (US$) |
|---|---|
| Platinum | $1,530/Ounce |
| Gold | $833/Ounce |
| Copper | $6,762/Metric Ton |
| Aluminum | $2,519/Metric Ton |
| Steel* | $661/Metric Ton |
| Coal* | $94/Metric Ton |
| Iron Ore* | $85/Metric Ton |
| Stone* | $8/Metric Ton |
| Sand & Gravel* | $6/Metric Ton |

*Steel is US HRC Import Price (FOB), Iron Ore is fines 67.5% iron content (FOB), Coal, Stone, and Sand & Gravel are US and Canadian regional prices.

Source: Global Financial Data; Thomson Datastream; Bloomberg Finance L.P.; International Monetary Fund; Government of British Columbia.

Note: Data as of 12/31/07.

Bulk materials with low value-to-weight ratios like coal, iron ore, lumber, and construction aggregate have the greatest regional disparities. Steel and specialty chemicals, with hundreds if not thousands of product variations and niche markets, can also have significant regional pricing disparity. Most precious and industrial metals, along with commodity chemicals, have relatively small disparities.

Basic materials with relatively small regional pricing differences are typically priced globally on commodity exchanges. Prices for products with greater regional differences are typically priced regionally upon sale by producers.

Iron ore is a notable exception. The majority of its prices are negotiated annually in year-long contracts between steel makers and miners. This helps provide stability for both highly capital intensive and cyclical industries. A spot market with prices set by regional producers does exist, but it's relatively small. Under the annual pricing system, the largest producers negotiate annual prices and smaller producers have little choice but to follow. In economic terms, this makes the large producers "price setters" and the small producers "price takers."

## My Year's Different Than Your Year

Annual iron ore contracts do not begin in January. Instead they begin at the start of Japan's fiscal year—April 1. Japan was historically the world's largest iron ore importer (China surpassed it in 2003), representing the steel industry in negotiations with iron ore producers.

In 2008, BHP Billiton (the world's third-largest iron producer) called for the elimination of annual price contracts, believing they didn't properly reflect supply and demand. While the firm eventually agreed to annual contracts, it's possible someday annual contracts will give way to a larger spot market or even pricing on an exchange.

*Source:* John D. Jorgenson and William S. Kirk, "Iron Ore," U.S. Geological Survey Minerals Yearbook (2003).

## Futures Exchanges

A commodity exchange provides a market for buyers and sellers to trade contracts of a physical commodity with a specified future delivery date. Because the delivery date is in the future, these exchanges are also commonly called *futures exchanges*. For example, on an exchange you could buy 100 tons of copper for delivery in three months, six months, two years, and so forth.

While contracts typically originate at set intervals starting at three months and going out as far as five to ten years, once the contract is created it trades on a daily basis until maturity. Figure 1.1 shows a graph of futures prices for copper at various maturities. In this case, investors expect the price to fall over time. They'll ultimately be proved right or wrong and the price of their contract will equal the going spot price upon maturity.

When the *futures curve* (also known as a forward curve for non-exchange traded commodities) is inverted and the future price is below the current price, the commodity is in *backwardation*, reflecting current scarcity relative to future expectations. When the futures curve is positively sloped and the future price is above the current price, prices are in *contango*, reflecting a surplus relative to future expectations. Because of storage, insurance, and financing costs, it's normal for non-perishable commodities to be in contango.

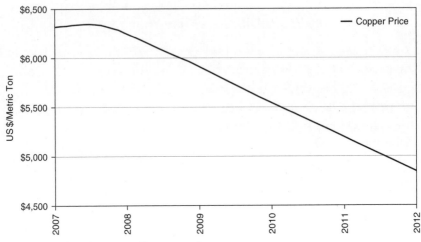

**Figure 1.1    Copper Futures Curve**
*Source:* Bloomberg Finance L.P. as of 12/31/07.

Modern futures exchanges originated with the Chicago Board of Trade in 1848. It was created to provide stability to Midwestern farmers' incomes. Without futures or forward contracts, a farmer's business is quite risky. A farmer invests substantial money in seeds, fertilizer, weed killers, machinery, and labor to grow and harvest crops, but doesn't know what the crop will sell for, even months after it's planted. By pre-selling the crop, the farmer knows exactly what can be spent along the way while still ensuring a profit. The futures market takes the price risk out of the equation. Taking risk out of the equation proved to be very popular and the Chicago Board of Trade quickly grew.

### Traditions at Work

Futures contracts for metals are sold in three-month intervals because in the late 1800s, it took about three months for Chilean copper to reach English ports. The three-month forward contract allowed merchants to hedge or protect themselves from the possibility of a fall in copper prices while merchandise was in transit.

*Source:* London Metal Exchange.

Speculators also engage in futures trading, although they rarely hold a contract to maturity and therefore don't take physical delivery of the good. Future exchanges like the London Metal Exchange (LME), the Chicago Board of Trade (CBOT), the Chicago Mercantile Exchange (CME), the New York Mercantile Exchange (NYMEX), and the New York Commodities Exchange (COMEX) all provide pricing information and venues for Materials trading.

Different commodity exchanges often specialize in different products. Chicago's commodity exchanges oversee greater volumes of agricultural-based commodities (tied to their history as an exchange for Midwestern farmers). The London Metal Exchange is historically the global leader in metals because England was first to experience an industrial revolution.

## THE PRODUCTION PROCESS

A good understanding of how basic materials are produced provides a foundation for further analysis and insights into costs, potential production bottlenecks, and other risks faced by producers. So let's look at the following basic life cycles:

- Metals
- Chemicals
- Concrete
- Paper

But first, some definitions.

### Upstream Versus Downstream

An operation is considered *upstream* if it is closer to the starting point of the production process—usually involving pulling actual raw material out of the ground. *Downstream* operations are closer to the finished product purchased by end consumers.

The terms stem from the metaphor of a stream or river. A river's flow starts upstream at its source and ends downstream. The closer the source, the farther upstream you are. In steel making, an iron ore mining operation is about as far upstream as you can go. By comparison, a steel producer is downstream and a steel distributor is even farther downstream. Upstream and downstream operations usually have very different margins, business models, and benefit from different economic environments. Vertically integrated producers have both upstream and downstream operations complementing each other.

## The Life Cycle of Metals

Unless you believe in medieval alchemy, you probably know metals come out of the ground. Finding them in commercially viable quantities and mining them with the proper approvals, however, is no easy trick.

**Finding Metal and Securing Permits.** The search for minerals begins far above the ground. Satellite imagery allows geologists to scan for appropriate topography and view regions under different wavelengths of light to find resource-rich sites—allowing for geological analysis otherwise invisible to the naked eye. Geologists then create detailed maps of the earth's mineral content based on the reflection and absorption properties of the clay, rock, soil, or vegetation of the terrain.[3]

Once a promising search area is discovered, the interested firm meets with the land owner (usually governments) to negotiate broad exploration or mineral rights covering wide territories, often tens of thousands of acres.[4] Governments typically negotiate contracts as leases with specific exploration and development time frames to ensure firms are actively investing in their country rather than speculatively purchasing rights to sell at a higher price in the future.

Geologists then survey and take samples to assess likely ore veins and identify spots for drilling exploratory holes. They often explore sparsely inhabited areas with no more than their packs, a donkey, and a few local guides. Based on the geologists' findings, firms drill exploratory holes. And with costs often over $300,000 to drill a 3,000 foot deep hole, the decision isn't made lightly.[5]

## The Long Arm of the Law Reaches Underground

In the legal world, "mineral rights" can be separated from "surface rights"—the right to anything, literally, on the land's surface. Owners wanting to retain use of their land and the buildings on it maintain surface rights and grant mineral rights to miners who want access, but don't want to pay for the buildings and any surface use.

All contracts vary, but they typically detail how the underground minerals can be extracted, the extent of the miner's right to surface use, and any reclamation by the miner to return damaged portions of the surface to their previous state. Most landowners sell their rights in some form rather than develop the resources themselves because mining is so highly capital intensive.

If a viable quantity of ore is discovered, the firm applies for government and environmental permits to construct a mine. Approval usually involves fees, royalty agreements based on a percent of revenue or mine production, taxes, and even mandated social programs for the community. (And sometimes a bit of backroom dealing with government officials.)

Such agreements are permanently binding only in theory. Governments have a funny habit of coming back for more and re-negotiating terms when it suits them. Additional fees and other alterations years later are not uncommon. A recent example is the dramatic changes to South African mining laws in 2004. Called the Black Economic Empowerment program (BEE), it addresses previous racial inequality under apartheid, but also represents a dramatic shift in ownership requirements. Existing mining companies must transfer 15 percent of ownership to individuals designated as historically disadvantaged South Africans by April 2009 and 26 percent of ownership by April 2014. South Africa also reviewed mining royalties and proposed significant changes on each type of metal.[6]

**Building a Mine.**    Once a viable metal deposit is identified and necessary permits obtained, a firm begins development. This is often a multi-billion dollar process depending on the size of the mine, necessary roads, rail lines, access to power and water, and the nearest shipping ports. (Because ore is heavy and mined in huge quantities—over 2 billion tons mined globally each year[7]—it's typically transported by rail and sea.) The largest mines can reach over two miles wide and a mile deep.

### Powering Mines Takes Serious Power

Mining is extremely power intensive. BHP Billiton forecasts its Australian Olympic Dam mining complex will require about 690 megawatts of power when development is completed around 2018. That's equivalent to over 40 percent of South Australia's electricity in 2007.

*Source:* Rebecca Keenan, "BHP Says Labor, Tool Shortages Strain Olympic Dam Update 2," Bloomberg (May 29, 2008).

New mining projects are known as "greenfield" projects because the project was started in an unspoiled "green field." Expansions to an existing mine or drilling at a nearby site is known as a "brownfield" project—a project commenced in a well-traveled area with established roads and infrastructure.

Brownfields typically represent less risk. Mineral rights are generally already established and the terrain is well understood. However, most brownfield regions with potential for significant ore deposits have already been explored, and current brownfield projects are typically smaller expansions. So although greenfield projects are much riskier, they often have the potential for much larger discoveries.

Mines can either be built underground or as open pits, depending on the depth and concentration of ore veins. Collapsing tunnels, toxic fumes, and operating heavy machinery in close quarters make underground mines significantly more dangerous. They typically have a conveyor belt system to transfer out rock and ore. Open pit mines involve blasting rock, loading it into large dump trucks, and hauling it out.

## The Benefits of Working in Open Pit Mines

South Africa has many of the world's deepest mines, reaching depths of over two miles. A study by the Leon Commission found an estimated 69,000 workers lost their lives in South Africa's mines from 1900 to 1994. Unfortunately, such incidents persist. In 2006 alone, South Africa's underground mines claimed 199 lives.

Not only are open pit mines much safer, but the dump trucks used are some of the most impressive vehicles in the world. The largest sport tires over 12 feet high, payload capacities of up to 380 tons, and a 24-cylinder, 3,500 horsepower engine under the hood. The nearby picture shows how massive these dump trucks and their tires are. These trucks often run continuous shifts, 24 hours a day, 7 days a week, trucking mined material to processing centers. Tires for these trucks can cost up to $40,000 each and burst with the force of up to 16 sticks of dynamite!

*Source:* Jeremy Roberts, "BHP's Olympic Dam Mine will Need Half of SA's Electricity," The Australian (March 27, 2008); Ndaba, "Can South Africa Stop Mine Deaths?" Mining Weekly (February 1, 2008); Caterpillar Inc. Press Release, "Power Train Simulators Put New Large Mining Trucks to the Test—Long Before They Hit the Haul Road," (September 2007).

### Liebherr T 282B Mining Truck
Courtesy of www.openstockphotography.org.

**Separating Metal from Rock.**    Mined rock is crushed smaller than the size of a dime and sent through a grinder, turning it into a fine powder. Then metal is separated from rock and minerals to create "concentrate."

Chemical flotation or leaching is typically used to create concentrate. The process involves a bath of water and a chemical reagent. When air is pumped into the solution, chemicals cause the ore to attach to rising air bubbles forming a surface froth that is skimmed off. This easily allows sorting multiple types of ore from the same batch of rock. Simply by changing the chemical composition of the bath, another ore type rises to the surface. Once skimmed, the material is filtered and dried to remove excess water and reduce shipping weight.

### Why Miners and Environmentalists Don't Always Get Along

Leaching poses some hefty environmental drawbacks. Per ton of rock, often less than a quarter ounce of precious metals and only 10 to 20 pounds of industrial metals are recovered. This means large water supplies are needed to process millions of pounds of metal each year.

In 2000, the US Geological Survey (USGS) estimated the US mining industry used approximately 3.5 billion gallons of water a day, or about 1 percent of the country's total water consumption. In addition to draining local water resources, mines must dispose of water along with leftover rock, called *tailings*. Since chemicals (such as cyanide and sulfuric acid) used to leach out the metals are often toxic, the tailings are often contaminated and can damage the surrounding environment if not properly disposed.

Because of this risk, mining firms are subject to strict environmental regulations and liable for clean-up costs and punitive penalties if they fail to comply. The permit requirements and potential costs of deviating from them increase the cost of doing business and serve as additional barriers to entry.

Concentrate is still not pure metal and requires additional refining or *smelting*. The metal percentage in concentrate (called *concentrate grade*) depends on the metal type, processing efficiency, and presence of other impurities. Copper concentrate for example typically only holds between 15 and 35 percent actual metal depending on the quality of the ore and efficiency of the leaching process.[8]

**Metal Smelting.**    Concentrate is typically created on site or in close proximity to a mine to reduce transportation costs. Once the metal has been processed into a concentrate, it's shipped to a smelter for further refining. Metal smelters are to the metal industry what oil refineries are to oil. Many firms specialize in either smelting or mining. For example, most Chinese copper firms mine very little of the metal and focus on smelting since copper is scarce in China but demand is high. Therefore, China imports vast amounts of copper concentrate, making it one of the world's largest copper smelters.

Smelters melt concentrate down and mix it with materials like limestone, which absorb impurities and leave a material with a 40 to 60 percent metal ratio called *matte*. Hot, oxygen-enriched air is blown through the molten matte to purify it over 95 percent and create *blister* (named for the air bubbles that form on the surface). The blister is then heated in an anode furnace to burn off excess oxygen and form *anodes*, which are 99 percent pure metal.[9]

While this quality level is usable for many purposes, some uses require 100 percent purity. Copper used in electrical wiring is further refined to maximize its electrical conductivity. To further refine it, the anodes are put through electrolysis. The metal is dissolved in a water and chemical bath and attracted to an electrically charged pole. As it dissolves and attaches to the pole, impurities left behind fall to the bottom of the tank, and the result is metal with 99.99 percent purity, called a *cathode*. The various stages of the smelting process are summarized in Table 1.3.

Refining differs slightly for each metal. Some metals like gold require little to no refining. Others like copper must undergo the full

### Table 1.3   Stages in Copper Smelting

| Stage in the Smelting Process | Metal Percentage |
| --- | --- |
| Concentrate | 15% to 35% |
| Matte | 40% to 60% |
| Blister | 95% to 98% |
| Anode | 99% |
| Cathode | 99.99% |

*Source:* US Environmental Protection Agency.

smelting process. Iron ore doesn't even use the basic leaching process in its transformation into refined iron (called pig iron) and then steel. There's also usually more than one way to refine a metal, but this is among the most common processes.

Smelting typically yields lower profit margins than mining. Smelters generally sign annual contracts to provide a stable flow of input materials. When global smelter capacity exceeds the supply of concentrate produced by the miners, negotiating power falls into the hands of miners and smelting fees decline. When the reverse occurs, smelting fees rise.

Smelters buy ore from miners at the daily London Metal Exchange (LME) benchmark rate, minus the amount of the annual pre-negotiated fee. Since annual contracts are long term, smelters typically negotiate what's known as *price participation*, allowing smelters to increase fees by a pre-determined level if prices exceed a certain threshold. For example, a smelter may charge $0.25 per pound to refine copper, with the agreement that for any period in which copper exceeds $4 per pound, the charge increases to $0.35 per pound.

In 2008, smelting capacity outpaced copper production from mines by such a large margin that miners eliminated the price participation clause and smelting fees dropped by 25 percent. That year, it cost $0.20 per pound to form anodes, and roughly another $0.05 per pound to further refine it into cathodes. These charges are called treatment (TC) and refining charges (RC), respectively, and often are denominated as TC/RC in shorthand for the total smelting fee.[10]

**Metal Recycling.** Metal can be recycled once its useful life has passed. Today, recycling is a $70 billion industry in the US alone. Two-thirds of the steel and a third of the aluminum produced in the US now comes from recycled scrap.[11] And recycling can mean significant energy savings, as seen in Table 1.4.

The US isn't the only energy-conserving country. In 2007 the US exported over 19 million metric tons of scrap metal to foreign countries. Emerging markets rank among the largest scrap importers, with China leading the way. Since most construction is brand-new in

**Table 1.4    Energy Savings From Recycling vs. Using New Ore**

| Metal | Energy Saved |
|-------|--------------|
| Aluminum | 95% |
| Copper | 85% |
| Steel | 74% |

Source: Institute of Scrap Recycling Industries.

developing regions, they are forced to import large quantities to realize the savings.[12]

## The Life Cycle of Chemicals

Chemicals and their products are pervasive—paints, glues, plastics, fabrics, lubricants, cleaners, and many others. Even the binding of this book is held together by a chemical adhesive! So how are they made?

First, a disclaimer: Detailing how thousands of different chemicals are made would require many encyclopedias, so the following description is simply a guide to typical chemical synthesis. But keep in mind the process won't apply to all chemicals.

A few products in the chemicals industry are mined, like potash and phosphate for fertilizer. But the majority of chemicals start with oil or natural gas. Once petroleum is out of the ground, its next step to becoming a finished chemical is through commodity chemical plants.

**Commodity Chemicals.**    Commodity chemicals are typically intermediate steps on the way to becoming final products. They are mass-produced in plants attempting to manufacture material of acceptable quality at the lowest possible cost.

End markets are huge, which makes competition fierce. A producer who can gain an edge and undercut its competitors stands to benefit tremendously. As competitors battle to gain efficiencies and drive down marginal costs, the size of the operation typically grows to exploit economies of scale. The commodity chemical industry is characterized by large manufacturing plants producing large volumes of chemicals at a steady rate. In fact, these plants often run 24 hours a day.

The most commonly used feedstock for commodity chemicals are naptha, a by-product of oil refining, and ethane, the second largest component of natural gas behind methane. Once isolated, these products go through a process called "cracking" to break down large hydrocarbons into smaller ones like ethylene and propylene.

Steam cracking is the most common process. Naptha or ethane is heated to over 750 degrees Celsius until a reaction occurs. Depending on the specifics of the input, scientists know the exact temperature the reaction will take place and stop it milliseconds after it starts. That short time, however, is enough to break down hydrocarbons, which are then filtered into ethylene, propylene, and other basic substances.

Ethylene and propylene are two of the most commonly used commodity chemicals because they are among the simplest forms of hydrocarbons in existence, making them extremely versatile for use as building blocks in specialty chemicals.

### The Secret Behind Fresh Produce

While ethylene is primarily used to create other chemicals, one of its few retail uses is as a ripening agent for fruits and vegetables.

**Specialty Chemicals.**    There are thousands of specialty chemicals filling countless niches for various products and purposes. Often, new chemicals are even developed by working directly with a specific customer to improve a single product, enter a new market, or increase efficiency. On a higher level, one of the biggest end markets is the industrial manufacturing sector.

While commodity chemical plants typically run continuously, specialty chemical plants produce ad hoc batches of chemicals with volume dependent on current customer needs. Since markets for specialty chemicals are smaller, competition is not as fierce. The gains from improving efficiencies and undercutting a competitor on a single chemical are relatively small and not worth large investments of time or capital. Pricing power is therefore strong, and the specialty chemical industry is much less cyclical than the commodity chemical industry.

**Overview of Chemical Production.**   In broad terms, the chemical-making process can be thought of as a tree. The trunk, commodity chemicals are the relatively few large branches that split off from the trunk, and specialty chemicals are the thousands of twigs that split from the main branches. As covered in greater detail in Chapter 4, the only force generally large enough to move all of them at the same time is economic growth.

**Chemical Recycling.**   Many chemicals cannot be recycled (such as household cleaning products), but plastics can be. In fact, recycling plastic is 80 percent more energy efficient than producing new plastic. In 2007, the US is estimated to have recycled 576,000 metric tons of used plastic bottles.[13] But that doesn't mean there isn't room for improvement. The Container Recycling Institute estimates only one-third of all plastic beverage containers in the US are recycled.

### The Life Cycle of Concrete

Whether used to lay a home's foundation, hold up walls, build a skyscraper, or pave a sidewalk, concrete is a vital component of the construction industry. In fact, concrete is the second most consumed substance on earth after water.[14]

Concrete is a mix of 80 percent construction aggregate (crushed rock) and 20 percent cement. Once water is added, cement remains malleable for a period before hardening into its final rock-like form.[15]

### I Speak Roman. Do You?

The Romans are considered to be the greatest users of concrete among ancient civilizations (though the Greeks and other societies also used it). Not only did they use it prolifically, but their use of fine volcanic sand made their concrete harder than previous versions—much of it still stands today. We owe the name *concrete* to the Roman term "concretus," meaning grown together or compounded.

**Making Construction Aggregate.** Construction aggregate has many grades or sizes, but can generally be separated into *fine* and *coarse*. Fine aggregate, like sand, is often dredged from lakes, rivers, or sea beds; while coarse aggregate, like gravel or crushed rock, is typically mined from quarries with explosives and broken down into various sizes by machines called crushers. Aggregate is quarried near its end market because its low value-to-weight ratio makes it too expensive to ship long distances. Gaining permits for quarries near large population centers can be difficult, since most communities don't want to be near a business that regularly sets off loud explosions. The aggregate used in concrete is typically about 60 percent gravel and 40 percent sand.[16]

**Making Cement.** The most commonly used cement is *Portland* cement, primarily a mix of limestone, clay, and sand, with about 85 percent of its final mass made up of lime and silica (the limestone mixture used to remove impurities in metals, called "slag," is often recycled in this mix as well).[17] The ingredients are ground to a fine powder, mixed in exact ratios, and placed in a furnace. While there are wet and dry methods of creating cement, most new furnaces are dry furnaces because they use less energy.

Dry cement furnaces are typically long rotating tubes, up to 12 feet in diameter (wide enough to drive a car through) and 400 feet long, set at a slight incline. The mixture is placed in the top of the furnace and slowly travels down the inclined and rotating tube while being heated to over 2,700 degrees Fahrenheit. Chemical reactions take place along the way and the result is marble-sized pieces of new material called clinker.

Clinker is ground into a fine powder and mixed with various additives, depending on the characteristics of the cement desired. Cement powder is ground so fine it can pass through a sieve capable of holding water.

Cement is primarily manufactured regionally due to its low value-to-weight ratio, but unlike construction aggregate, some global trade does exist. In 2005, the US imported approximately 28 percent of its cement, with most going to coastal regions like California.[18] However, the US is expected to expand its cement production capacity by 27 percent between 2007 and 2012 to replace the higher cost imports.[19]

### Alternative Uses for Your Kitchen Stove

The discovery of Portland cement is generally credited to a British stone mason named Joseph Aspdin in 1824. He invented the substance by baking a mixture of limestone and clay in his kitchen stove before grinding it into a fine powder. He is said to have called it Portland cement because it looked like a stone quarried on the Isle of Portland off the British coast.

*Source:* Portland Cement Association.

Heating the large cement furnaces to high temperatures is very energy intensive. It takes about a half pound of coal to produce one pound of cement. Over 1.6 billion tons of cement is produced globally each year—that's a lot of coal.[20]

**Concrete Recycling.** Over 140 million tons of concrete are recycled each year—the most recycled material in the US by weight. Once cement bonds with water, its chemical properties change and can't easily be returned to its old use. Recycled concrete is often used as filler in place of crushed rock. Its most common end market is providing a foundation for roads.[21]

### The Life Cycle of Paper

Paper, of course, starts with trees. For our purposes, trees can be segmented into two categories: *hardwoods* and *softwoods.*

### The World Runs on Paper

On average, over 120 pounds of paper per year are consumed for every person on earth! In the developed world, the annual consumption rate is even higher at an average of 661 pounds per person.* While it depends on the type and size of the tree along with the type of paper being made, it's estimated one ton of paper takes between 12 and 24 trees to produce.

*"Wood for Paper: Fiber Sourcing in the Global Pulp and Paper Industry," Seneca Creek Associates, LLC and Wood Resources International, LLC, (December 2007).
*Source:* Conservatree (www.conservatree.com).

**Cutting Lumber.**    Hardwoods are primarily used as veneer, furniture, cabinets, flooring, doors, and other specialized interior applications. Examples of hardwoods are walnut, maple, oak, cherry, elm, and beech. These woods are typically too valuable to be used for paper and are sent to sawmills to be turned into lumber, but the leftover scrap is often used in the paper industry. About 40 percent of US timberland is composed of hardwood timber, which has given rise to the largest hardwood sawmilling and processing industry in the world.[22]

Softwoods are primarily used as lumber for construction and to make paper. The largest end market for softwood lumber is the residential housing market. Examples of softwood are pine, Douglas fir, and redwood. Wood used for paper production is called pulpwood and results from diseased or heavily branched softwood trees unusable for making lumber, the scraps from sawmills, and a few trees such as eucalyptus, which are widely grown specifically for pulpwood.

### Urban Sprawl Meets Its Match

About a third of the US is covered in forest land, and there are an estimated 20 percent more trees in the US today than 25 years ago.

*Source:* American Forest & Paper Association.

Forest land owners have a variety of harvesting methods, including clear-cutting (where every tree is cut down), diameter limit cuts (where any tree over a specified diameter is cut), and selective harvests (where only designated trees are cut). One of the most commonly used methods is a variation of the selective cut called a "group selection" harvest.

In a group selection harvest, small patches of forest, up to about an acre in size, are cut in scattered fashion throughout the forest. Most forests in highly regulated areas are cut using the selective or group selective method because they are considered the most sustainable practices. To help sustainability, new young trees are planted in place of the removed mature trees to help the forest re-grow.

Most trees planted specifically for lumber or paper are given an 8- to 15-year life cycle prior to harvest, but it varies depending on the tree and climate. Trees can be felled by hand with chainsaws or much more efficiently and safely with tree harvesters. Tree harvesters are somewhat like large tractor capable of grabbing a mature tree, felling it, shearing its limbs, cutting it to the desired length, and stacking it for transport at a rate of about 45 trees per hour.[23]

**Processing Paper.**    Once lumber is cut and delivered to a paper factory, the paper-making process has only just begun. Wood is first put through rollers to remove any bark and then ground down into small chips. The chips are placed in large tanks and boiled at high temperatures with sodium hydroxide and sodium sulfide. This breaks the wood down into pulp and dissolves the lignin (the natural glue holding the wood together), leaving behind cellulose fibers.

In most cases, the pulp is bleached white and put through a process called "beating," which mashes the pulp. At this point, fillers like chalk and starch are added, affecting the final opaqueness and paper quality. Then pulp is laid on a fine mesh screen and subjected to rollers, pressing water out through the screen, leaving behind compressed pulp. Despite attempts to recycle its water when possible, the pulp and paper industry is the single largest industrial water consumer in the developed world.[24]

The pulp sheet is pressed into form and sent over a number of hollow, heated rollers to dry the paper. At this point, pigments or latex finishes may be added for color patterns or a glossy coat depending on its intended use. The final result is a sheet of intertwined cellulose fibers we call paper. No glue is used in the process. Because of all those steps, the paper industry is one of the most capital intensive industries in the world.

### The Origins of Paper

The invention of paper is typically credited to a Chinese court official around 100 AD. He is thought to have mixed mulberry bark, hemp, and rags into a pulp before pressing out the liquid and hanging it to dry. However, paper makers didn't successfully begin using wood fiber for mass production until the 1800s.

*Source:* American Forest & Paper Association.

**Paper Recycling.** Used paper can be recycled very affordably. In fact, the most expensive part of recycling paper is gathering it. Recycled paper is dissolved in a chemical bath to turn it back into pulp, filtered to remove the additives, and then re-processed just like normal paper.

Besides reducing landfill size, recycling paper also has the advantage of taking 64 percent less energy to produce than making it from scratch.[25] The amount of paper recycled in the US has increased an impressive 87 percent from 1990 to 2007, with 56 percent of the paper consumed in the US in 2007 being recycled. This equates to nearly 360 pounds of paper recycled for every man, woman, and child in the US!

There is a limit, however, to our ability to recycle paper. Paper can only be recycled five to eight times before the fibers become too short and weak to be reused.[26] Nonetheless, approximately 36 percent of US paper production (including exports) is now made from recycled paper.[27]

## Chapter Recap

Now you have the foundation and basic tools to begin greater analysis of the Materials sector. You'll continue to see the processes in this chapter pop up throughout this book and a solid understanding of them is critical to analyzing the sector in greater depth.

- The Materials sector is made up of metals, chemicals, paper, lumber, cement, construction aggregate, and packaging.
- The sector is extremely capital intensive, often requiring tremendous initial investments of hundreds of millions or billions of dollars to start a business.
- The sector's capital intensity creates large barriers to entry, provides pricing power, and encourages consolidation into large dominant firms that maximize economies of scale.
- The sector is extremely economically sensitive.
- Pricing of its products (and any free market good) is always determined by supply and demand.
- Basic materials are priced either globally or regionally depending on how economical it is to ship them. This is typically determined by their value-to-weight ratio.

# 2

# A BRIEF HISTORY OF
# MATERIALS

John Templeton once famously said, "The four most dangerous words in investing are 'This time it's different.'" History never perfectly repeats, but it does have a habit of turning out similarly—so understanding it can provide key investing context and insights into the future. A history of the Materials sector could go back thousands of years. We could start with Stone Age Neanderthals throwing their first spears! But for the purpose of becoming better Materials investors, we'll start with the Industrial Revolution, focusing on the metal and chemical industries.

## THE INDUSTRIAL REVOLUTION

Henry Bessemer's creation of high-grade steel in the late 1850s kicked the Industrial Revolution into high gear, changing the world forever. His quest actually began after he invented a new type of artillery shell, but the cast iron guns of the day weren't strong enough to handle the more powerful ordnance. Changing raw iron ore into strong and malleable steel that could be mass-produced also allowed new inventions like steam engines, railroads, skyscrapers, and assembly-line manufacturing.

Previously, raw iron ore was traditionally melted by burning charcoal. This process produced carbon emissions absorbed by the raw ore to become usable iron. However, charcoal-making was soon deemed unsustainable because of massive deforestation in Britain. Coal appeared the obvious replacement, but its high sulfur content resulted in very brittle metals. In the early 1700s, the discovery of *coke* solved the problem. Coke is coal burnt in the absence of air the same way charcoal is made by burning wood in the absence of air. Limestone added to the mix removed additional impurities. The result was cast iron. By today's standards, with 4 percent carbon, cast iron is still quite brittle (the higher the percentage of carbon, the more brittle the iron or steel). But Bessemer revolutionized the industry by observing that blowing hot air through molten cast iron caused carbon to burn off, allowing the steelmaker greater control over carbon content. This led to mass production of cheap, high-grade steel in what are now known as Bessemer furnaces. Improvements on the original design yielded modern day blast and basic oxygen furnaces. Almost all steel today contains less than 2 percent carbon—considerably stronger and less brittle than pre-Bessemer cast iron.

Following Bessemer's breakthrough, a whole universe of machinery development and infrastructure construction became possible. Productivity skyrocketed, setting the stage for a dramatic increase in living standards over the next century.

The US and global steel industry boomed during this revolutionary period. Factories and cities sprang up to take advantage of this newly abundant material. One of the most revolutionary new industries dramatically affecting world development was railroads. Railroads transported goods and people cheaper, farther, faster, and in greater quantity than ever before. Federal land grants enabled US railroads to grow at a mind-boggling pace. At the end of the Civil War in 1865, roughly 35,000 miles of track existed in the US. By 1900, an estimated 192,000 miles of track had been laid.[1]

The introduction of mass-produced strong steel impacted almost every aspect of life. At the turn of the century, 41 percent of the nation's workforce worked in agriculture. Thirty years later, the portion roughly halved to 22 percent. Laborers were steadily pushed out of the fields by more efficient machinery and followed new opportunities into growing cities. By 2000, America's agricultural workforce totaled just 2 percent.[2] A similar process is happening today in emerging markets like China and India. Such tremendous change and growth also produced tremendous wealth (especially in the steel industry). Many of America's most legendary businessmen made fortunes in iron and steel, including Andrew Carnegie and JP Morgan.

## An M&A Blast From the Past

JP Morgan formed US Steel through the merger of Carnegie Steel Company and the Federal Steel Company in 1901. The company represented 7 percent of US GDP, produced two-thirds of the country's steel, and supplied nearly a third of the world's steel. It was also the world's first company worth $1 billion, with an initial market capitalization of $1.4 billion.

*Source:* U.S. Steel Kosice, "History," (September 2003).

Despite a massive increase in consumption, most metal prices did not spike upwards during the Industrial Revolution. While prices did rise, the pace was relatively well contained as supply increased practically as quickly as demand. From 1880 to 1910, US steel production increased from 1.3 million tons to more than 24 million, making the US the world's largest steel producer. Dramatic increases in productivity during this time also lowered production costs for raw materials, helping further moderate prices. These productivity gains can be seen in Figure 2.1, which shows the inflation-adjusted, or *real,* price of aluminum from 1910 through 2007. Other than a price spike during World War I, real aluminum prices have declined dramatically over time, falling 70 percent due to lower production costs. In fact, prior to harnessing cheap energy in the Industrial Revolution, aluminum was actually one of the most precious

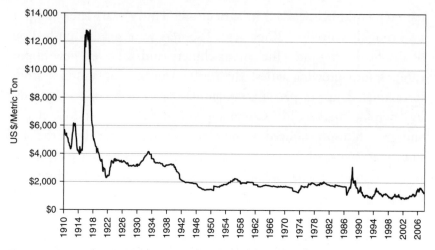

## Figure 2.1    Real Aluminum Prices 1910–2007

Source: Global Financial Data.

metals on earth. The top of the Washington Monument is capped with aluminum because, in the late 1800s, it was more precious than gold.

## The Birth of the Modern Chemicals Industry

As energy became readily available and industrialization thrived, Chemicals was among the first new industries to emerge. Though it's hard today to imagine life without plastics, the first synthetic plastic, Bakelite, was only developed in 1907. Bakelite was heavily used in the growing auto and radio industries. Cellophane soon followed. Then DuPont scientists forever changed the industry with their discoveries of neoprene (a synthetic rubber), nylon (a synthetic fiber), and Teflon (a non-stick coating and the slipperiest substance on earth). The industry continued to grow throughout the twentieth century with countless variations of new additives, lubricants, adhesives, and plastics. Among them were distinctive new classes of carbon fibers in the late 1950s and synthetic fibers called Kevlar in the 1960s.

Historically, the Chemicals industry's growth has hinged on innovation. This includes developing new materials and finding new applications for existing ones. Teflon, for example, was used in various

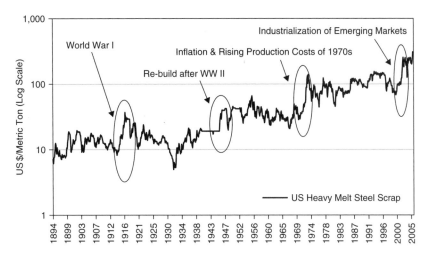

**Figure 2.2    US Scrap Steel Prices**
*Source:* Global Financial Data.

industrial processes for over a decade, including the Manhattan Project in 1941, before it made its way into consumer products like pots and pans in the 1950s. The ubiquitous yellow sticky Post-it Note is another classic example of innovation creating a new product market. The weak adhesive pasted to the back of each note was actually a failed attempt at creating super strong glue. It ended up on the pages of a hymnal church book to mark pages without damaging them. From that, a new adhesive market was created.

## STRUCTURAL SHIFTS IN METALS SINCE THE INDUSTRIAL REVOLUTION

Since the Industrial Revolution, the world market for basic metals has experienced four primary periods of dramatically advancing prices—the mobilization for World War I, the re-build after World War II, the inflationary period of the 1970s, and the recent industrialization of the emerging markets. (The price resurgence after the Great Depression was more a reflection of the end of deflation and return to normalcy than a structural shift or massive new demand.) Figure 2.2 illustrates these historic structural shifts by looking at US scrap steel prices.

## The Surge of World War I

The Industrial Revolution had been in progress for a few decades by the time World War I broke out, and the world didn't hesitate to employ its newfound technologies. The world shifted its manufacturing base to mass-produce machines of war. The tools of modern warfare were born: armor, poison gases, and heavy artillery became commonplace. Tremendous demand for many metals drove prices higher—Figure 2.3 shows the price of scrap steel and copper during the period.

## Re-Building After World War II

During World War II, much of Europe's infrastructure was leveled—countless roads, bridges, manufacturing plants—even entire cities—were destroyed. Japan was similarly damaged. Heavy bombing destroyed over 50 percent of Tokyo, and atomic bombs devastated Hiroshima and Nagasaki. Following World War II, the US was virtually the only major industrialized country to remain (essentially) unscathed. Its industrial and infrastructure systems remained intact and were in fact greatly

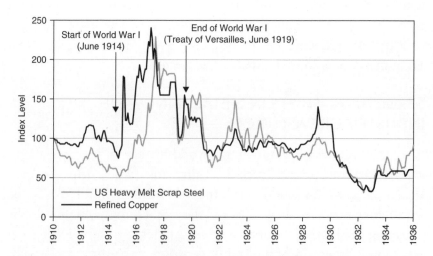

**Figure 2.3    Copper and US Scrap Steel Prices 1910–1935**
*Source:* Global Financial Data.
*Note:* Data indexed to 100 as of 12/31/1909.

bolstered as a result of the war effort. The rest of the developed world had to rebuild—the global demand for steel products was unprecedented. If Materials usage was high during the war, the rebuilding process saw even greater demand, and the US was the linchpin. In 1950, the US produced nearly 50 percent of the world's steel.[3] America's competitive advantage allowed it to quickly reconfigure its wartime manufacturing base to make consumer goods, resulting in a surge of economic growth.

This growth translated into tremendous performance for metals stocks. Figure 2.4 shows the performance of S&P Steel industry stocks over the 20-year period after World War II. Starting in early 1949, it surged 564 percent over the next 10-and-a-half years before leveling off again.

### Inflation of the 1970s

Surging global inflation in the 1970s represents the next period of significant Materials growth. For the first time, it wasn't all about economic growth. Instead, investors saw raw materials as a shelter from inflation's erosive effects. Concurrent with the increase in broad-based

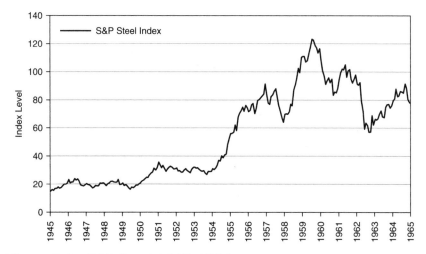

## Figure 2.4    S&P Steel 1945–1964
*Source:* Global Financial Data.

inflation, that decade's oil shocks led to a dramatic increase in energy costs and therefore higher production costs for many materials.

---

### The Rise of the Mini-Mills

Up until the 1970s, steel was largely made in blast furnaces following the same basic methods Henry Bessemer discovered back in the 1850s. Because of skyrocketing oil prices, however, engineers had a tremendous incentive to develop more energy efficient production processes. The result was the mini-mill.

The first mini-mill was conceived in the 1960s but didn't become viable until energy costs climbed higher in the 1970s. A mini-mill is smaller than a normal steel plant and melts scrap steel in an electric arc furnace rather than making it from raw iron in a blast furnace.

Due to the nature of the production process, traditional blast furnaces typically run continuously and can take weeks to shut down or start up. Mini-mills not only require significantly less energy, but can also be built on a smaller scale and be turned on or off at will. This reduces fixed costs, allows for regional production (reducing shipping costs), and allows volume adjustments according to customer demand. Early mini-mills largely avoided using unionized labor, giving them an advantage in labor costs as well.

US steel production has remained relatively flat since the 1970s at around 100 million tons a year, but mini-mills now account for over 50 percent of production.

*Source:* Leslie Wayne, "Parched, Big Steel Goes to Its Washington Well," *New York Times* (January 20, 2002).

---

**Fall of the Gold Standard.** Inflation is simply an excessive increase in money supply that doesn't get absorbed by the economy. One of the reasons inflation took hold so strongly during the 1970s was the abandonment of the *gold standard* in 1971.

The gold standard was adopted by most nations after World War II. According to the Bretton Woods Agreements, most countries pegged their currencies to the US dollar, and the US promised to fix the price of gold at $35 per ounce. Thus, the amount of fiat (paper) money governments could print was constrained because its value was directly tied to an unchanging amount of gold. This policy helped protect the US (and all the countries pegged to its currency)

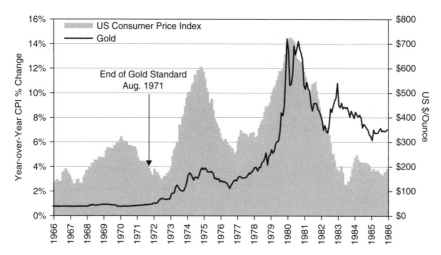

**Figure 2.5    Gold Prices vs. US Inflation 1966–1985**

*Source:* US Bureau of Labor Statistics; Global Financial Data.

from mismanaging their money supplies and creating excessive inflation. However, it also restricted each nation's flexibility to support the economy through monetary policy adjustments.

In 1971, the world abandoned the gold standard for a fiat money system. The constraint preventing governments from endlessly increasing money supply as they saw fit was removed and inflation soared. Gold and other precious metals skyrocketed because they were viewed by many as better stores of value than paper money. Figure 2.5 shows gold prices and US inflation from 1966 through 1985. Inflation skyrocketed following the end of the gold standard, and gold peaked in 1980. However, better central banking globally helped tame inflation through the end of the 1980s and onward; gold would not reach those price levels again until 2007. Chapter 4 will cover gold and its drivers in more depth.

## INDUSTRIALIZATION OF THE EMERGING MARKETS

With communism's decline and the failure of socialist economies in the late 1980s and early 1990s, the world's developing economies began to embrace the capitalistic western model. Emerging markets today

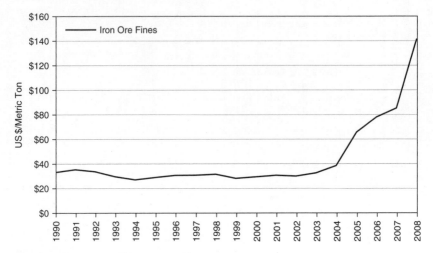

**Figure 2.6    Iron Ore Benchmark Prices**
Source: International Monetary Fund.

are responsible for much of the tremendous growth in consumption of steel, iron, copper, and other industrial metals over the last decade. This trend can be attributed to enormous wealth increases in heavily populated countries with limited existing infrastructure bases.

Figure 2.6 shows an example of the strain this structural shift has placed on commodity prices. The price of iron ore fell 2 percent from 1990 to 2003, but increased 340 percent from 2003 to 2008 as emerging market infrastructure building kicked into high gear.

But it's not just emerging markets that are consuming commodities. The developed world simultaneously requires a massive rebuild of its aging infrastructure. For example, the American Society of Civil Engineers recently assessed the condition of America's infrastructure and gave it a "D." Repairs to modernize America's infrastructure are estimated to cost about $1.6 trillion and take about five years.[4]

The combination of initial investment in the rapidly growing emerging markets and accelerating re-investment in the developed world has placed a strain on raw material supply. Chapter 6 will cover the drivers and consequences of these forces in greater detail.

## Chapter Recap

While history doesn't perfectly repeat itself, understanding the past provides context for future events. The Industrial Revolution changed the Materials sector forever—harnessing energy and the ability to mass-produce steel set off a series of events, creating tremendous demand for metals and chemicals. Since that period, every global war and large-scale industrialization has led to a surge in the Materials sector and its largest industry, Metals & Mining.

- The Industrial Revolution dramatically lowered production costs and expanded consumption of basic materials.
- The modern chemical industry was simultaneously born and has experienced steady growth throughout the last century, predicated on the development of new products and end markets for its products.
- World War I created a surge in metal consumption.
- World War II and the re-build of Europe and Japan following the war again spurred tremendous growth in metal demand.
- The high inflationary period of the 1970s created a flight to safety in commodities.
- The industrialization of emerging markets recently created a dramatic new upturn in the sector.

# 3

# MATERIALS SECTOR DRIVERS

Simply looking for the best stock is the most common investor mistake. That may sound counterintuitive, but it's true. Unless you've got a firm grasp on a sector's fundamental drivers and how they impact industries and ultimately individual firms, it's a near hopeless task to choose the right stocks. High-level sector drivers often have equal, if not greater, influence on a stock's performance than unique firm-specific fundamentals, so accurately identifying sector drivers is a must.

Every sector has unique drivers relative to the broader economy, and they're not static—they constantly change. What's vital in 2008 for Materials may not be exactly the same in 2010. Nevertheless, the factors described in this chapter were chosen because they are relatively timeless and serve as a good starting point for any Materials analysis, regardless of the investing environment.

We can't cover every detail of every portion of the sector—that warrants an encyclopedia, not a book. Instead, the focus will be primarily on metals and chemicals, because (as Chapter 4 will cover in greater detail) they comprise the majority of the sector and carry the most relative weight.

Note: Understanding the drivers won't give you direct instructions on how to invest. Investing environments shift too quickly for any definitive "rules" for all time. Rather, it's about critical thinking. Understanding sector drivers is more like a road map providing the tools and resources to make your own analysis on a forward-looking basis. This chapter covers the most important drivers and provides the necessary tools to begin analyzing the sector.

## KEY DRIVERS

Though the list below is by no means comprehensive, the most important Materials drivers include:

1. Economic growth
2. Commodity prices
3. Commodity production growth
4. Exploration and development costs
5. Production costs
6. Share buybacks and mergers and acquisitions (M&A) activity
7. Investor sentiment
8. Taxes, politics, and regulations

Let's explore these drivers in a bit more detail.

### Economic Growth

As mentioned in Chapter 1, economic growth is one of the dominant Materials demand drivers. For example, by looking at global GDP per capita and per capita expenditure on basic materials and (particularly) metals, we know there's almost a direct correlation—higher economic output leads to increased basic material consumption. As the developing world continues industrializing and global GDP per capita increases, the demand for basic materials will increase dramatically.

## Commodity Prices

Commodity prices are usually the most influential factor on Materials company earnings and stock market performance. Remember, a stock is nothing more than partial ownership in a business. As a stockholder and owner, the larger the earnings and the longer you can generate them into the future, the better. With a limited amount of resources in your mine, quarry, or on your land, and high fixed costs throughout the sector, prices typically impact earnings the most.

As covered in Chapter 1, basic material prices (like any market-based good) are determined by supply and demand. Long-term supply and demand, however, is tremendously difficult to predict and not helpful when making investment decisions. Therefore, it's typically better to focus on the near-term supply and demand environment, typically 12 to 18 months in the future (as you should do for stock-specific decisions in general). At any given time, other factors can overwhelm price impact for a specific producer or region, but commodity prices generally are the most significant Materials driver.

### Media Myths—A Weak Dollar and Global Materials Consumption

Because most basic materials are priced in US dollars, the media often argues a weak US dollar makes them cheaper outside the US, which in turn spurs additional consumption. That's not really true.

The truth is a weak dollar may cause prices of globally consumed basic materials to rise from the US standpoint, but it doesn't necessarily change the quantity demanded or consumed. Underlying supply and demand can remain unchanged regardless of what currencies do. In other words, if all other currencies were to strengthen 100 percent against the US dollar and the underlying supply and demand of a basic material priced globally in US dollars did not change, the material's price should increase 100 percent in US dollars and 0 percent in all other currencies. Such a move doesn't add to consumption, and the price movement is simply a difference in currencies.

## Commodity Production Growth

Production growth is generally a good thing, but for upstream companies producing raw materials it can be a double-edged sword: more production means higher sales in the short term, but also increased depletion rates. After all, no mine is inexhaustible.

Production growth is also frequently firm-specific and may not apply across an entire industry or the sector as a whole. The rate at which resources are used up and/or replaced, however, is a key issue for individual firms and in determining industry supply.

## Exploration and Development Costs

Costs associated with finding new materials sources for mining have an effect on long-term supply and production, but have limited impact on all the current production already in place. Why? Because it generally takes years and tremendous resources to discover a new mine and develop it to a point where it actually begins regularly producing a material like iron ore, gold, or copper. That means exploration and development is imperative for valuing a company over the long term, but it won't affect prices much in the short term.

## Production Costs

Earnings are basically sales minus costs. Therefore, production costs play a major role in determining any firm's profitability.

In the short term, firms farther downstream in the production process focused on processing raw materials (such as steel or chemical producers) are more sensitive to input cost changes than upstream miners. Processors must constantly purchase their input, giving them more variable costs, whereas miners just purchase the land once, making those costs relatively fixed. The cost per pound of metal produced by a miner can fluctuate with a mine's production volume, but that is generally firm-specific rather than an industry- or sector-wide force.

## Share Buybacks and M&A Activity

This principle holds for any sector, not just Materials: As firms buy each other at a premium, it often causes similar firms' valuations to rise in anticipation they too might get bought. The acquisition premium paid can also ripple throughout an industry as investors use it to gauge what industry insiders (who theoretically know the industry's prospects better than anyone else) see as a fair valuation for similar firms. Thus, a sector undergoing a lot of consolidation will often see rising share prices.

## Investor Sentiment

Investor sentiment can be a powerful but fickle force in any economic sector. It can cause huge stock price swings (think "bubble") or modest price fluctuations. Therefore, being on the right side of sentiment swings can be crucial. No perfect sentiment indicator exists, but industry valuations and the media can provide some context. Recurring media stories can provide a window into investors' moods and interests.

But don't be fooled. Positive sentiment isn't necessarily good, and negative sentiment isn't automatically bad. If sentiment is negative, it can improve, which can be a positive driver and vice versa. Sentiment at its extremes can often indicate a sector's fortunes are about to change dramatically. For example, extreme euphoria is usually a good sign there's little upward buying pressure left, and stock prices may fall dramatically.

## Taxes, Politics, and Regulations

Royalty taxes, import and export taxes, price caps, subsidies, permit approvals, and other forms of legislation can be significant drivers. Increasing taxes and regulations can seriously hurt profitability, while decreased taxes and deregulation can provide an earnings boost.

Taxes and regulations vary country by country and typically change quickly at the whim of politicians. We can't cover them all in the space allowed by this book, and any list provided would soon be outdated. However, the next few chapters cover several examples demonstrating regulatory and legislative impact.

Regulations in China, the US, and Europe often have a magnified effect on the sector because of their large consumption of basic materials. For regionally priced goods, regulations in the pertinent region are also important.

### Inflation's Impact on Commodities

Higher inflation is often considered a demand driver for basic materials and metals. The theory is investors look for a stable and tangible store of value outside paper money in an inflationary environment. Non-perishable commodities fit the bill since they derive their value from their physical usefulness, regardless of the amount of money printed.

Outside of the precious metals, however, inflation is rarely a significant driver of end demand. In most basic materials, final purchasers taking delivery of the good are almost exclusively industrial users.

Ultimately, inflation is, always and everywhere, a monetary phenomenon and historically has to reach extreme levels (such as in the 1970s) to cause investors to seek protection by significantly shifting into raw material producers.

## DRIVERS AT WORK

We've covered the sector's main drivers, but they're only a broad outline of what to look for. To better analyze any basic material industry and its components, we will drill down into some tangible fundamental questions that should be answered.

### Is the Material Priced Globally or Regionally?

Knowing how a material is priced provides key insights into its drivers, potential supply constraints, and how to analyze it further. Generally speaking, producers of globally priced goods should be evaluated globally, and producers of regionally priced goods should be evaluated regionally. (As covered in Chapter 1, global versus regional pricing is determined by the economics of shipping the material.)

Global trends and competitors play a major role in industries with globally priced materials. Regional events have less impact on those industries, unless the regional events have far-reaching global consequences. This isn't to say a regional event like a new tax law can't affect a single producer, but its impact on the overall industry only extends as far as its ability to impact the global environment.

On the other hand, regional events obviously play a major role in industries where materials are priced regionally. And the more regional the pricing, the less affected the industry will be by global events. For example, it's almost never economical to ship construction aggregate long distances. This causes distinct regional pricing differences and means construction aggregate should be evaluated purely on a regional basis. By comparison, steel is also priced regionally, but different grades can be economical to ship to certain markets and significant trade in steel does take place. Therefore global events can impact producers, and analysis shouldn't be limited to regional factors alone.

### What Is the Material Used For?

Understanding end use helps determine the specific demand drivers for any basic material. For example, you might think jewelry would be the primary determinant of platinum consumption. But no! Actually, catalytic converters used for filtering car exhaust account for over 55 percent of platinum use.[1] So when investing in a platinum producer, you'll want to pay attention to trends in global auto growth.

### Who Are the Primary Consumers?

Who's buying, and how much? For instance, knowing that China consumes about two times more iron ore and copper than the next closest country means you can logically focus on China as a primary driver for those metals. (China consumes a bit over 40 percent of all iron ore and close to 25 percent of all copper.)[2]

## Where Is It Produced?

This question gets to the heart of geopolitical risks to supply. It's vital to understand trade, working conditions, government intervention (and in some cases, nationalization), and other regional factors. For example, about 80 percent of all platinum production is in South Africa.[3] Early in 2008 when Eskom (the state-owned utility responsible for providing 95 percent of South Africa's electricity) cut power to most of the country and shut down the country's mines, global platinum prices spiked as production dropped.[4]

## Who Are the Largest Producers?

Knowing the largest players helps identify which companies to track as bellwethers for industry trends. If investing in specific firms, it also identifies competitors and allows for strategic attribute comparisons. This is important because it can determine relative future performance and uncover any potential production bottlenecks the other questions fail to identify.

## What Are Production's Primary Costs?

Understanding the primary cost of production helps identify any risk factors likely to shrink margins. This could include fuel, labor, or raw material costs—depending on the industry and region. When answering this question, it's also important to look for structural competitive advantages some producers might have over others.

For example, two primary inputs for steel producers are iron ore and coking coal. In 2008, when annual iron ore costs increased over 65 percent and coal prices increased over 200 percent, producers who did not have their own source of raw materials saw margins shrink as they struggled to pass through the higher costs.[5]

## Are There Significant Barriers to Entry?

The higher the barrier to entry, the harder it is for competition to enter the market—a huge competitive advantage for those already in the game. Identifying barriers to entry will also generally highlight the obstacles current producers face in expanding their own production over time.

For example, the iron ore industry has extremely large barriers to entry due to limited high-quality deposits and extremely high start-up costs. As a bulk good with a low value-to-weight ratio situated a long distance from its customers (due to the limited regional availability of deposits), start-up costs typically include not only a mine, but also a railroad and port for transporting ore to customers. These factors have led the industry to consolidate into a small group of large producers to maximize economies of scale, with the largest three controlling 75 percent of global iron ore trade (as measured by seaborne trade).

### Scarcity Power

Economists often argue profits are simply a representation of scarcity power: the ability to provide something others can't at that price. If others can just as easily offer the same good at the same price, then competition is fierce, and prices and earnings typically drop until some form of scarcity power is re-gained. This is especially true in the Materials sector, where scarcity of a raw material is a crucial determinant of prices.

## What Is the Expected Change in Supply and Demand?

As covered in Chapter 1, supply and demand forces determine prices. Given the importance of prices and production growth to this sector, understanding expected supply and demand forecasts is critical for any Materials industry. After all, much of a producer's or industry's stock market returns hinges on whether prices and production growth are above or below expectations.

To see why, recall that markets are generally efficient discounters of known information. You must know what others expect and compare your own analysis to it. If you and everyone else believe copper supply will remain flat while demand will go up 5 percent next year, it won't help you much. It doesn't mean you're necessarily wrong, but being right won't win you anything since that information is already widely known and discounted into prices. But if everyone else expects demand to go up 5 percent, and believe that estimate is too high or low, you can make a market bet based on your different expectations. To understand the risk and potential benefit of your position, you must know what others expect.

Future supply and demand forecasts of most basic materials can easily be found through trade publications (some examples are listed in Appendix A). Given the long lead times for development of new mines or processing plants, major increases in supply can usually be anticipated and are rarely a surprise. The primary exception to this is when technology suddenly changes (as discussed in Chapter 1, relative to nickel supplies during 2007). By comparison, supply shortfalls from labor strikes, power outages, equipment failures, natural disasters, and a host of other potential bottlenecks regularly surprise investors and are very difficult to accurately predict. Changes in demand are often a result of economic growth or contraction in an industry's end markets.

It's crucial to understand the difference between demand and consumption. In principle, consumption can't exceed production and the two should match, excepting leftover inventories. The question we're concerned with is at what price will this match occur? This is controlled by production (supply) and the desired consumption at a given price (demand). The price will adjust until the desired consumption matches the production.

Note: When forecasting prices, don't worry about the exact price forecast—there's almost no way to be that precise. More important than forecasting an exact price is understanding whether prices will be above or below *consensus expectations*.

Consensus future price expectations of globally priced exchange-traded materials can be found using futures curves. Technically futures curves are proxies for consensus expectations—you need to adjust slightly for costs such as storage, insurance, and financing. But for our general purposes, and throughout the rest of this book, we will treat them as guides to consensus expectations. Recall from Chapter 1 that futures curves show expected future prices over varying lengths of time. Ultimately understanding what is expected is vital to determining whether the reality will end up better or worse than expectations and the industry's stocks will rise or fall.

## Prices Are Determined at the Margin

Despite millions of barrels of oil or hundreds of thousands of pounds of copper being traded each day by thousands of people, the pricing of these goods is determined by only a handful of people. Not to worry, this isn't a vast conspiracy. It's just good-old supply and demand hard at work.

In a free market controlled by supply and demand, changes in prices are determined on the margin. In other words, the value of a good is determined each day by the final two people who want it. One will end up with the good and the other will not. The value of the good is the point at which that final individual agrees to forego it.

For example, consider a situation where 10 people desperately want a good and exactly 10 units exist. Prices will be low since no one is forced to go without it. By adding an eleventh person, however, prices would suddenly skyrocket as they bid against each other until a price is reached where someone agrees to do without it. This has important consequences because it means that depending on the price elasticity of the good (how sensitive consumption is to changing prices), large fluctuations in production or desired consumption are not necessarily required for prices to move significantly.

## CASE STUDY: COPPER

Let's put these questions into practice by looking at just one material—copper. At nearly 30 percent, copper makes up the largest percentage of revenue of any metal within the mining industry—more than twice as much as the next material. (We'll further break down the mining industry by relevant metals in Chapter 4.)

Copper is the third most abundantly produced metal in the world behind iron ore and aluminum.[6] Long before it was discovered to be a useful electrical conductor, it played a role in improving standards of living. In fact, the harnessing of its properties was so important, we named a whole time period around it: The Bronze Age.

## Is Copper Priced Globally or Regionally?

Because copper is a commodity with a relatively high value-to-weight ratio (outlined in Chapter 1 in Table 1.1), it can be economically shipped and is therefore priced globally on commodity exchanges around the world. Because it is priced globally, it must be evaluated on a global basis.

## What Is Copper Used For?

Copper has the highest electrical conductivity of any metal outside of the prohibitively expensive precious metals (silver's actually the best electrical conductor), and about 75 percent of total copper usage is for copper wire.[7] It's also heavily used in plumbing and pipes because of its corrosion-resistant properties. Due to the combination of wiring, pipes, roofing, and other aesthetic uses, building construction is copper's largest single end market, consuming about 50 percent of all copper.[8] (For a more detailed breakdown of copper usage, check the London Metal Exchange's website at www.lme.co.uk/copper_industryusage.asp.)

---

### Copper Trivia

- Archaeological evidence points to copper use as far back as 10,000 years ago. The discovery of alloying it with tin led to the Bronze Age, around 4,500 years ago.
- When Columbus sailed to America, his ships had copper skins below the water line to extend the hulls' lives and protect against barnacles. Today, most vessels use a copper-based paint to protect the hull.
- In 2005, 34 percent of global copper consumption came from recycling. As with most metals, copper can be recycled with no effect on its properties or performance.

*Sources:* "Copper History," International Copper Association (2007), International Copper Study Group, "The World Copper Factbook 2007"

## Who Consumes Copper?

Today, the emerging markets make up slightly over 50 percent of total copper consumption, with China leading the way at over 20 percent. China was responsible for an estimated 60 percent of the demand growth from 1997 to 2007 and is the driving force behind the increase in global consumption.[9] As shown in Figure 3.1, the US is a distant second in total consumption at 12 percent, followed by Germany and Japan. No other country consumes over 5 percent.

Emerging markets development and future increases in global GDP per capita mean copper consumption can also be expected to grow. Figure 3.2 shows the correlation in copper consumption per capita and GDP per capita by country. As a country increases in wealth and industrializes, it also increases its use of electricity or power. This requires vast amounts of electrical or copper wiring. So

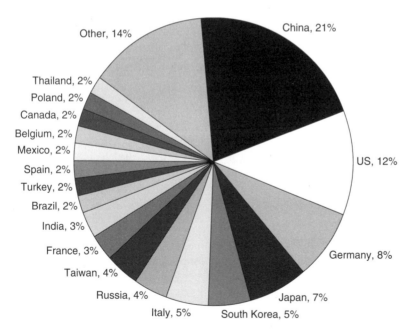

### Figure 3.1   Global Copper Consumption by Country
*Source:* International Copper Study Group: The World Copper Fact Book 2007
*Note:* Sum exceeds 100 percent due to rounding.

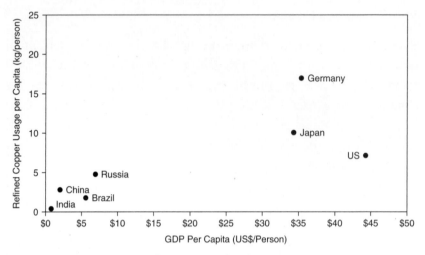

**Figure 3.2   Intensity of Copper Use by Country**

Source: International Copper Study Group: The World Copper Fact Book 2007; International Monetary Fund; US Census Bureau.

Note: Data is for full year 2006.

while the US currently uses more than twice as much copper per person as China, the gap is narrowing.

In fact, if global consumption simply continues to grow at the same 3 percent annual rate we've seen since 1960, the world will need to produce over 700 million metric tons of copper over the 30-year period from 2008–2037.[10] That's more copper than has been mined to date!

---

### A Penny for Your Thoughts

Though typically thought of as mostly copper, a US penny is only 2.5 percent copper and 97.5 percent zinc. The penny retains its bronze hue due to the fact it was once 100 percent copper and varied from 90 to 100 percent copper until 1982, when it was changed to its present formula. One notable exception was in 1943, when pennies were produced with zinc-plated steel to conserve copper for the war effort of World War II.

Interestingly, the other silver-hued coins are primarily copper:

- A nickel is 75 percent copper and 25 percent nickel.
- A dime is 91.7 percent copper and 8.3 percent nickel.
- A quarter is 91.7 percent copper and 8.3 percent nickel.

Source: US Mint.

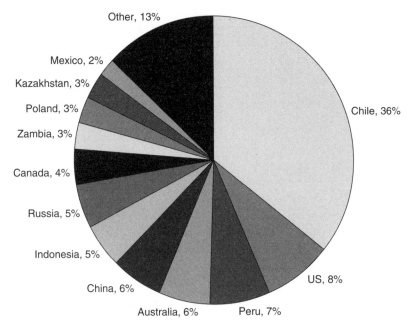

**Figure 3.3   Global Copper Production by Country**

Source: International Copper Study Group: The World Copper Fact Book 2007

Note: Sum exceeds 100 percent due to rounding.

## Where Is Copper Produced?

An estimated 36 percent of all copper is produced in Chile, making it a closely watched country for copper analysts. As shown in Figure 3.3, the US is a very distant second while Chile's neighbor Peru is third. With nearly 45 percent of global copper production dependent on one South American region, national labor strikes, earthquakes, power outages, legislation, and regulations can have a significant impact on copper supplies and prices.

## Who Are the Largest Copper Producers?

The largest copper producers and their 2007 production totals are listed in Table 3.1. Codelco is the largest producer, but is privately owned by the Chilean government. Notice how prominently four of the top five diversified metals and mining companies place in the

## Table 3.1   2007 Top 10 Copper Producers

| Producer | Production (Thousand Metric Tons) |
|---|---|
| 1. Codelco (state owned by Chile) | 1,665 |
| 2. Freeport-McMoRan Copper & Gold | 1,583 |
| 3. BHP Billiton Ltd. | 1,391 |
| 4. Xstrata Plc | 931 |
| 5. Rio Tinto | 738 |
| 6. Anglo American Plc | 666 |
| 7. Grupo Mexico SAB* | 592 |
| 8. KGHM Polska Miedz SA | 441 |
| 9. OAO GMK Norilsk Nickel | 423 |
| 10. Kazakhmys Plc | 348 |

*Southern Copper is majority owned by Grupo Mexico and excluded to avoid double counting.
Source: Bloomberg Finance L.P.

rankings (BHP, Rio Tinto, Xstrata, and Anglo American). Given the industry's concentration (covered in greater detail in Chapter 4), you'll find at least one if not all four of these companies (along with Brazilian heavyweight Vale) near the top of almost any metal (or coal) production list.

## What Are the Primary Costs Associated With Copper Production?

Specific costs for all mining companies vary depending on the countries they're located in, labor agreements, access to power supplies, royalty agreements, and so on. For example, a miner with operations in the developed world will likely have higher labor costs than a miner in emerging markets. Figure 3.4 breaks out the costs for Southern Copper, one of the largest and relatively pure copper producers (most major producers are diversified miners), with mines in Mexico and Peru. The cost breakdown shows miners are significant

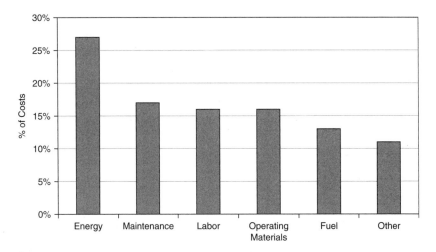

**Figure 3.4    2007 Southern Copper Cost Breakdown**
*Source:* Southern Copper: May 2008, Overview & Highlights of Company Presentation.

energy consumers with about 40 percent of the company's total costs devoted to power and fuel.

## Are There Any Significant Barriers to Entry in Copper?

Large barriers to entry exist in mining metals, including copper. They include government permits, high capital costs, instability of labor contracts, long construction lead times (often 5 to 10 years), backlogs to gain access to necessary equipment, and of course difficulty in simply finding new mines.

In the words of Richard Adkerson, the CEO of Freeport McMoran (the largest publicly traded copper producer in the world), on why he made the bold move in early 2007 to acquire larger rival Phelps Dodge, "We understood just how difficult it is in today's world to produce copper from aging mines and also to find new supplies of copper."[11]

Remember, barriers to entry not only deter new entrants from entering the market, but can also create many of the largest obstacles facing current producers—preventing them from significantly expanding production.

Normally, as prices rise, new mines that were uneconomical at the old price because of lower-grade ore (less metal per ton of rock) or a higher-cost structure are brought online to boost supply. This helps moderate prices over time. However, when extremely high barriers to entry exist, production may be slow to increase, allowing prices and earnings to rapidly accelerate.

This has recently been the case with copper—a large supply increase is unlikely through at least 2010. In response to a question posed in early 2008 about what might cause copper prices to decline, Mr. Adkerson responded, "It's not going to occur as a result of supply side factors. The supply side situation in terms of current production levels and new projects coming on stream continue to be very supportive of the copper price."[12]

## What Is the Expected Change in the Supply and Demand of Copper?

As previously discussed, predicting consumption and demand (desired consumption at a given price) are two different things. Figure 3.5 shows differences in production and consumption since 1960, along with copper prices. Copper prices fluctuated widely despite nearly identical growth in mined copper production and refined consumption (the difference is largely inventories and recycled material). Prices are the best measure of the interaction of supply and demand in a free market system.

Predicting prices or both production (supply) and desired consumption (demand) is extremely difficult, and analysts regularly miss forecasts by wide margins (again why you shouldn't focus on making specific forecasts. Remember: What matters is your general forecast relative to expectations). For example, most analysts consistently underestimated copper prices as the emerging markets began to industrialize and copper prices surged.

Future copper price expectations can be seen using a copper futures curve (which we analyzed in Figure 1.1). Recall the curve was declining, demonstrating investors at the time expected copper prices to decline in the future. During most of the surge in the Materials sector from 2003 through 2007, the futures curve was inverted as investors expected copper prices to decline from their highs.

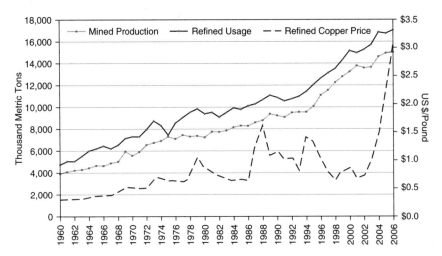

**Figure 3.5  Copper Production & Consumption with Copper Wire Prices**

*Source:* International Copper Study Group: The World Copper Fact Book 2007; Global Financial Data.

Prices, however, remained high due to stronger-than-expected demand from the emerging markets and a host of supply disruptions. Because prices remained higher than expected, the stock prices of copper producers increased significantly as investors adjusted to the higher-than-expected earnings. If copper prices had fallen below expectations, copper producers' stock prices would have likely declined as investors adjusted to lower-than-expected earnings.

You can find future prices through major exchanges such as the NYMEX or LME. The following link is for copper futures, but similar information exists for other metals as well: www.nymex.com/cop_fut_csf.aspx.

## Copper Summary

You should now have a basic understanding of copper, its producers, and drivers:

- Copper is primarily used for electrical purposes (both in buildings and machines).

- It's sensitive to economic growth, and its consumption increases with per capita GDP as societies industrialize.
- China is currently its primary demand driver; Chile is currently its primary supply driver.
- Fuel and energy are some of its largest production costs.
- Large barriers to entry exist for new competition.

This information can be used to craft your opinion about future copper prices and copper producers' earnings, which can be compared to general price expectations using a futures curve. If you expect future copper prices and producers' earnings to be above current expectations, stock prices can be expected to rise, and you may want to overweight copper producers within your portfolio (hold a greater weight than your benchmark).

As we'll discuss in greater detail in Chapter 7, no decision to overweight an industry or sector should be made in a vacuum. Instead, it should be made relative to your beliefs about other industries and sectors.

## Chapter Recap

You should now be familiar with Materials basic drivers and equipped with a set of questions to help analyze any material in greater detail. Of course, no book can outline every possible driver and its relative importance at a given point in time, but with a little common sense and knowing the right questions to ask, you're well on your way to making informed decisions about the sector.

- Economic growth is the primary demand driver for goods produced in the Materials sector, and material prices are generally the most important determinant of earnings across an industry.
- While earnings of raw material producers benefit from rising raw material prices, processors such as the steel and chemical industries depend primarily on the spread between raw material inputs and prices for final goods.
- The more uneconomical it is to ship a good, the more regionally it is priced, and the more regionally the industry should be evaluated.

- Supply and demand always determines prices in a free market. Differences in expectations and reality of future supply and demand will determine prices, drive earnings, and be a primary determinant in long-term stock performance.
- Outside of earnings, other factors such as M&A and sentiment can affect performance.
- Questions to ask when analyzing a material include:
  - Is the material priced globally or regionally?
  - What is the material used for?
  - Who are the primary consumers?
  - Where is it produced?
  - Who are the largest producers?
  - What are the primary costs associated with production?
  - Are there any barriers to entry?
  - What is the expected supply and demand growth?

# II

# NEXT STEPS: MATERIALS DETAILS

# 4

# MATERIALS SECTOR BREAKDOWN

**N**ow you've got the basics of how the Materials sector works, an understanding of its history, and its high-level drivers. But a high-level understanding is just the beginning. Just like our overall economy, each sector is made of many distinct parts—some are relatively similar to others and some are quite unique. To better understand the whole, you must understand the parts.

Chapter 1 covered the basic categories of the Materials sector: metals, chemicals, construction materials, and paper. But that's really an oversimplification—all the metals and chemicals have unique characteristics and drivers. This is also true of the other Materials industries and the sub-industries that comprise them.

Before making any portfolio decision, you must understand what makes each distinct sector component tick. This chapter explores the sector's sub-industries and how an investor can form an opinion on each.

## GLOBAL INDUSTRY CLASSIFICATION STANDARD (GICS)

Before beginning, some definitions: The Global Industry Classification Standard (GICS) is a widely accepted framework for classifying companies into groups based on similarities. The GICS structure consists of 10 sectors, 24 industry groups, 68 industries, and 154 sub-industries. This structure offers four levels of hierarchy, ranging from the most general sector to the most specialized sub-industry:

- Sector
- Industry group
- Industry
- Sub-industry

Let's start by breaking down Materials into its different components. According to GICS, the Materials sector consists of one industry group (Materials), five industries, and 15 sub-industries. Below are Materials' industries and corresponding sub-industries.

Metals & Mining

- Diversified Metals & Mining
- Steel
- Gold
- Aluminum
- Precious Metals & Minerals

Chemicals

- Commodity Chemicals
- Specialty Chemicals
- Diversified Chemicals
- Fertilizers & Agricultural Chemicals
- Industrial Gases

Construction Materials

- Construction Materials

Paper & Forest Products

- Paper Products
- Forest Products

Containers & Packaging

- Paper Packaging
- Metal & Glass Containers

## GLOBAL MATERIALS BENCHMARKS

What's a benchmark? What does it do, and why is it necessary? A benchmark is your guide for building a stock portfolio. You can use any well-constructed index as a benchmark—examples are in Table 4.1.

### Table 4.1    Benchmark Differences

| Sector | MSCI World (Developed World) | MSCI EAFE (Developed World ex-US) | S&P 500 (Large Cap US) | Russell 2000 (Small Cap US) | MSCI Emerging Markets (Emerging Markets) |
|---|---|---|---|---|---|
| Consumer Discretionary | 9.8% | 10.8% | 8.5% | 13.5% | 4.9% |
| Consumer Staples | 8.8% | 8.5% | 10.2% | 3.0% | 4.2% |
| Energy | 10.9% | 7.9% | 12.9% | 6.7% | 18.0% |
| Financials | 22.6% | 26.9% | 17.6% | 18.9% | 21.7% |
| Health Care | 8.7% | 6.3% | 12.0% | 14.5% | 1.6% |
| Industrials | 11.4% | 12.1% | 11.5% | 15.1% | 9.7% |
| Information Technology | 11.0% | 5.5% | 16.7% | 18.3% | 10.1% |
| **Materials** | **7.2%** | **9.9%** | **3.3%** | **5.6%** | **14.7%** |
| Telecommunication Services | 4.9% | 6.2% | 3.6% | 1.5% | 11.5% |
| Utilities | 4.7% | 5.9% | 3.6% | 3.0% | 3.5% |
| **Total** | **100.0%** | **100.0%** | **100.0%** | **100.0%** | **100.0%** |

*Source:* Thomson Datastream; MSCI, Inc.[1] as of 12/31/07.

By studying a benchmark's makeup, investors can assign expected risk and return to make underweight and overweight decisions for each industry. This is just as true for a sector as it is for the broader stock market, and there are many potential Materials sector benchmarks to choose from. (Benchmarks will be further explored with the top-down method in Chapter 7.)

## Differences in Benchmarks

So what does the Materials investment universe look like? It depends on the benchmark, so choose carefully! The US Materials sector looks very different from Europe, Japan, and the emerging markets. Table 4.1 shows major domestic and international benchmark indexes and the percentage weight of each sector.

Sector weights show each sector's relative importance in driving overall index performance. While Materials is the third largest weight in the MSCI Emerging Markets index, it's the smallest weight of any sector in the US-based S&P 500. Why do Materials have more relative weight in emerging markets? Given a wealth of natural resources, but a lack of infrastructure and discretionary income to support other sectors, emerging markets typically have larger Energy and Materials sector weights than developed countries.

Since the weights are representative of the underlying sector and regions' structures, the weights aren't fixed and can change over time because of performance differences, additions and deletions of firms to the indexes, and a variety of other factors. For example, Financials wasn't always the biggest in most indexes. For many decades, Industrials dominated.

Understanding how your benchmark and the sectors within it are structured is crucial to developing a portfolio, since wide deviations in weightings can exist across regions and benchmarks. For example, in some countries, Materials is by far the largest sector; while in others, it's barely a few percent. Table 4.2 shows the Materials sector's weight in selected countries, based on the MSCI All Country World Index. Note the stark differences between developed and emerging market countries. For example, Peru's stock market is dominated by

## Table 4.2    Materials Weights by Country

| Country | Weight (%) |
| --- | --- |
| Peru | 76.6 |
| Brazil | 29.9 |
| Australia | 24.5 |
| South Africa | 21.1 |
| Mexico | 17.2 |
| Canada | 16.8 |
| Germany | 14.9 |
| UK | 10.8 |
| Russia | 10.7 |
| France | 9.1 |
| India | 7.9 |
| China | 6.9 |
| US | 3.5 |
| Spain | 0.6 |
| Italy | 0.4 |

*Source:* Thomson Datastream; MSCI, Inc.[2] as of 12/31/07.

Materials—mainly mining firms—but the big, diverse US market is near the bottom of the list with only a 3.5 percent Materials weight.

Not only can sector weights vary, but so can industry weights—sometimes greatly, depending on the chosen benchmark. Table 4.3 shows the weight of each Materials industry within each benchmark.

Understanding these weights allows you to not only properly weight your portfolio relative to your benchmark, but also effectively utilize your time by focusing on the most important components. (And for this reason, this book focuses more on the two largest industries—Metals & Mining and Chemicals—and less on the smallest industry—Containers & Packaging.)

Metals & Mining is the largest Materials industry in most broad global and non-US benchmarks. Because the industry is concentrated in dominant foreign mining firms, it has a much smaller US weight

**Table 4.3    Materials Industry Weights**

| Industry | MSCI World | MSCI EAFE | S&P 500 | Russell 2000 | MSCI Emerging Markets |
|---|---|---|---|---|---|
| Metals & Mining | **51.2%** | **56.6%** | 31.5% | 30.4% | **72.3%** |
| Chemicals | 37.4% | 32.3% | **54.9%** | **48.5%** | 14.0% |
| Construction Materials | 5.2% | 6.8% | 2.0% | 3.5% | 9.8% |
| Paper & Forest Products | 4.2% | 3.2% | 8.2% | 6.1% | 3.5% |
| Containers & Packaging | 2.0% | 1.2% | 3.4% | 11.5% | 0.5% |
| **Total** | 100% | 100% | 100% | 100% | 100% |

*Source:* Thomson Datastream; MSCI, Inc.[3] as of 12/31/07.

(Chemicals hold the largest US weight). The Metals & Mining industry also has less impact on small cap indexes (like the Russell 2000) because much of its weight is concentrated in larger firms. This wasn't always the case, but as machines have replaced manual labor and fixed costs have risen as a percentage of total costs, the benefits of economies of scale have grown and so have the firms.

It's important to consider regional composition as well. In a top-down context, local economic and political conditions have a large impact on sector, industry, and sub-industry performance. For example, if the US outperforms, that bodes well for the Chemicals, Paper & Forest Products, and Containers & Packaging industries—all with large US weights relative to the rest of the sector. For a similar reason, if the emerging markets outperform, Metals & Mining and Construction Materials should benefit. Using the MSCI All Country World Index (ACWI), Table 4.4 shows the regional distribution of global Materials industries.

Table 4.5 further breaks down sector sub-industry weights (largest weights by index are bolded). Gold made a lot of headlines in 2007 and 2008, but note it makes up just 0.4 percent of the MSCI World Index and 6.1 percent of the MSCI World Materials sector. It's an

## Table 4.4    Materials Industries by Regions

| Industry | Developed World Ex-US | Emerging Markets | US | Total |
|---|---|---|---|---|
| Metals & Mining | 60.4% | 27.0% | 9.3% | 100% |
| Chemicals | 58.3% | 8.9% | 30.7% | 100% |
| Construction Materials | 37.6% | 32.9% | 8.8% | 100% |
| Paper & Forest Products | 63.7% | 17.7% | 36.9% | 100% |
| Containers & Packaging | 45.4% | 6.0% | 56.4% | 100% |

*Source:* Thomson Datastream; MSCI, Inc.[4] as of 12/31/07.

even smaller weight in most other benchmarks. You could ignore gold altogether and not significantly impact your ability to outperform most Materials benchmarks.

Diversified Metals & Mining has the most impact in global indexes, because it contains firms producing copper, iron ore, and coal, the three largest revenue sources for global mining companies.

Notice how the structure of industries described in Chapter 1 influences the weightings across indexes in Table 4.5. For example, Commodity Chemicals has its greatest weight in Emerging Markets and Specialty Chemicals has its greatest weight in the small cap Russell 2000 Index. Can you guess why? Because commodity chemicals are priced globally and compete fiercely on production costs, producers have migrated to regions with the lowest cost of production. By comparison, specialty chemicals are priced regionally and serve niche markets, so a host of small regional producers exist.

### Even Broad Indexes Have Cracks

Stock market indexes only track publicly listed firms in designated countries. No index tracks every firm. Some of the largest holders of natural resources in the world are governments, and others are in very small markets that most indexes do not include. This means some of the world's largest mineral producers are not reflected in most, if any,

*(Continued)*

stock market indexes. For example, Codelco, the largest copper producer in the world, is owned by the government of Chile and not included in any indexes. Saudi Basic Industries, the world's largest chemical company, is based in Saudi Arabia and included in very few of the broadest global indexes.

## A Concentrated Group

When determining your over- and underweights to the benchmark for the Materials sector, it's important to have an opinion on (or at least knowledge of) the sector's largest companies. Recall from Chapter 1

### Table 4.5    Materials Sub-Industry Weights

| Sub-Industry | MSCI World | MSCI EAFE | S&P 500 | Russell 2000 | MSCI Emerging Markets |
|---|---|---|---|---|---|
| Diversified Metals & Mining | **28.3%** | **36.2%** | 9.7% | 7.4% | **32.0%** |
| Steel | 14.0% | 17.9% | 9.4% | 11.2% | 26.4% |
| Gold | 6.1% | 1.0% | 5.2% | 1.3% | 5.9% |
| Aluminum | 2.4% | 1.2% | 7.2% | 3.9% | 1.3% |
| Precious Metals & Minerals | 0.5% | 0.3% | 0.0% | 6.6% | 6.7% |
| Commodity Chemicals | 2.5% | 2.9% | 0.0% | 4.0% | 9.5% |
| Specialty Chemicals | 5.9% | 6.7% | 6.2% | **22.8%** | 0.0% |
| Diversified Chemicals | 15.3% | 15.6% | **22.9%** | 6.4% | 0.7% |
| Fertilizers & Agricultural Chemicals | 8.5% | 3.2% | 14.3% | 15.3% | 3.8% |
| Industrial Gases | 5.1% | 4.0% | 11.5% | 0.0% | 0.0% |
| Construction Materials | 5.2% | 6.8% | 2.0% | 3.5% | 9.8% |
| Paper Products | 3.3% | 3.2% | 4.6% | 5.3% | 3.4% |
| Forest Products | 1.0% | 0.0% | 3.6% | 0.8% | 0.1% |
| Paper Packaging | 0.8% | 0.6% | 1.5% | 1.8% | 0.3% |
| Metal & Glass Containers | 1.2% | 0.6% | 1.9% | 9.7% | 0.2% |
| **Total** | 100% | 100% | 100% | 100% | 100% |

*Source:* Thomson Datastream; MSCI, Inc.[5] as of 12/31/07.

that size matters because the sector is capital intensive in nature, leading to groups of dominant firms in each industry dwarfing their peers.

Table 4.6 shows the percentage the 10 largest firms make up in each Materials industry of the MSCI All Country World Index. With concentrations ranging from 45 to 85 percent of the industry, the largest firms truly dominate. A complete listing of the 10 largest firms in each Materials industry of the MSCI All Country World Index can be found in Appendix B.

It's important to understand the structure of the largest firms in each industry to help make over- and underweight decisions within the sector, but if you don't have the time for that, you should at least familiarize yourself with the largest firms in the sector. Based on the MSCI All Country World Index, Table 4.7 highlights the 10 largest Materials firms in the world. These 10 companies make up an impressive 30 percent of the sector's weight in the index.

Now that you have an understanding of how the sector is structured, let's use the questions we learned in the last chapter to briefly analyze each industry and its components.

In the following analysis, when a material is priced globally, we have also listed where you can find its future price expectations (recall from Chapter 3 it's your forecast relative to expectations that matters). Regionally priced materials typically lack the same simplistic pricing transparency, but regional producers often release their prices and forecasts in quarterly earnings reports or presentations found on company websites.

### Table 4.6   Concentration of Materials Industries

| Industry | Concentration of 10 Largest Firms |
| --- | --- |
| Chemicals | 45% |
| Metals & Mining | 48% |
| Construction Materials | 64% |
| Paper & Forest Products | 73% |
| Containers & Packaging | 85% |

Source: Thomson Datastream; MSCI, Inc.[6] as of 12/31/07.

Table 4.7    The 10 Largest Materials Firms in the World

| Company | Sub-Industry | Market Cap (Millions US$) |
|---|---|---|
| BHP Billiton | Diversified Metals & Mining | $186,988 |
| Rio Tinto | Diversified Metals & Mining | $159,277 |
| Cia Vale Do Rio Doce | Diversified Metals & Mining | $154,681 |
| Arcelor-Mittal | Steel | $112,669 |
| Anglo American Plc | Diversified Metals & Mining | $81,060 |
| BASF Ag | Diversified Chemicals | $71,862 |
| Xstrata PLC | Metals & Mining | $68,664 |
| Monsanto Co | Fertilizers & Agricultural Chemicals | $61,073 |
| POSCO | Steel | $53,557 |
| MMC Norilsk Nickel | Diversified Metals & Mining | $50,516 |

Source: Thomson Datastream; MSCI, Inc.[7] as of 12/31/07.

## Looking for Value

Investors typically classify stocks into the major valuation categories: *growth* or *value*. Growth stocks typically have higher valuations (usually price-to-earnings (P/E) ratios, but you could use a variety of metrics), while value stocks typically have lower valuations. The difference is subjective and frankly rather arbitrary. What one person may consider growth, another may consider value, and the classification can change for any single stock. Ultimately, it's important to remember neither category does better than the other in the long run, with value stocks leading during some periods (2003 to 2006) and growth stocks leading in others (1997 to 1999).

By most measurements, Materials stocks are generally considered *value*, though it can shift around. Investors are typically unwilling to grant Materials stocks very high valuations because of the sector's extreme cyclicality. All else being equal, if you expect value to take leadership over growth, the Materials sector is often a good sector to consider overweighting.

## METALS & MINING INDUSTRY

Now that you know the general sector breakdown, we can examine the industries in greater detail. First up: Metals & Mining. Metals & Mining firms produce copper, iron ore, steel, aluminum, nickel, zinc,

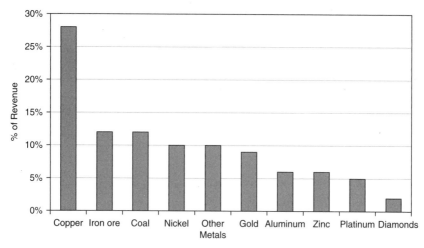

**Figure 4.1    2007 Revenue by Product of Top 40 Mining Firms**
*Source:* "Mine: As good as it gets?" Price Waterhouse Coopers

uranium, lead, gold, silver, platinum, and virtually any other metal you can think of, plus coal and diamonds. But as you can see in Figure 4.1, some materials are more important to the industry, and therefore to investors, than others. Figure 4.1 shows the percent of revenue generated by some of the largest metals in the mining industry.

Figure 4.1 shows only 40 of the largest firms, but still provides a good representation of what's important overall because the industry is so concentrated. In fact, the four biggest firms represent 43 percent of the group's revenue and 47 percent of the earnings.[8]

### Aluminum: Bigger Than It Seems

Relative to its overall industry importance, aluminum is underrepresented in Figure 4.1. This is because the chart is representative of the mining industry. Aluminum (similar to steel), however, is actually a *processed* metal and doesn't occur naturally in metallic form. Diversified miners generate some revenue from aluminum operations, but pure aluminum producers are represented in their own sub-industry.

Copper was covered in the last chapter, so now let's look at this industry's other major materials and their unique attributes. They include:

- Iron ore
- Coal
- Steel
- Gold
- Aluminum
- Nickel
- Zinc

All are priced (and should be evaluated) globally, with the exception of steel and coal, which have varying degrees of regional traits. Producers of these materials also have two basic business models: processors (steel and aluminum) and miners (virtually everything else).

### Iron Ore

Iron ore may be a one-trick pony—98 percent goes to steel production[9]—but modern civilization wouldn't have gotten very far without it. Massive quantities are required for construction, manufacturing, transportation, and consumer goods. The world now mines over 1.8 billion metric tons of iron ore a year—the weight of about 4,900 Empire State Buildings.[10] In fact, we consume so much steel that by physical weight, iron ore—and the steel it's transformed into—made up 95 percent of all metal produced in 2007.[11]

### Three Types of Iron Ore

There are three types of iron ore: fines (60 percent of global production), lumps (20 percent), and pellets (20 percent). While they are all priced on annual contracts as described in Chapter 1, pellets are the most valuable, followed by lumps, and then fines. Fines are pulverized pieces smaller than a grain of wheat, lumps are grain- to golf ball–sized pieces, and pellets are semi-processed with higher iron content. Media-listed generic annual iron ore benchmark prices are usually in reference to fines.

*Source:* Cleveland-Cliffs.

Just a few nations are blessed with high-grade iron deposits. In 2006, Brazil, China, and Australia were responsible for about 60 percent of global production. Significant volumes are exported to meet global demand because of regional scarcity. This makes transportation infrastructure—railroads, ports, and ships—as important as mines in determining total production. Fixed costs involved in building mines and related infrastructure are enormous, creating a high barrier to entry and making economies of scale crucial. These factors also create significant pricing power and a high degree of concentration. For example, in 2006, the top three producers (Vale, BHP Billiton, & Rio Tinto) controlled roughly 35 percent of global production and 75 percent of global exports.[12] (A full breakdown of regional production and consumption can be found in the Iron Ore Minerals Yearbook, produced annually by the US Geological Survey (USGS), at http://minerals.usgs.gov/minerals/pubs/commodity/iron_ore.)

## No Rush With Slow Transport

The reason gold rushes have occurred throughout history (but never a coal or iron ore rush) is because of the high fixed costs involved in transporting the ore. The lower the fixed cost, the easier (all else being equal) it is for competition to enter the marketplace. Consider the California Gold Rush of the 1840s. All it took was a bucket and shovel, and you could be a prospector. The payoff on a cheaper bulk commodity, however, is not worth your trouble unless you can gain economies of scale and maximize volume.

**Price Expectations** Because iron ore isn't traded on a futures exchange, no futures curve exists to easily determine investors' price expectations. But if you have a brokerage account, most major brokerages can provide their analysts' iron ore price forecasts. Another method is to look at global steel production forecasts. Increased steel production translates directly into increased iron ore consumption because steel production is iron ore's only significant use. Just remember not all steel is made from scratch—in 2006, about 70 percent of steel was made from iron ore and the other 30 percent was made from recycled scrap.[13]

## Coal

Coal is primarily used for power generation, steel production, cement production, and general industrial use. The vast majority, however, is used for power generation. Coal remains the most commonly used fuel globally—in 2007, an estimated 65 percent of coal production was used for power generation, providing roughly 40 percent of the world's electricity.[14]

Similar to iron ore, coal is a bulk good, with over five billion metric tons of coal consumed globally each year—more than twice as much as iron ore. Therefore it has many similar characteristics, including annual pricing contracts. However, because it's relatively abundant globally, production is fragmented by comparison, and pricing contracts are often negotiated on a regional or firm-specific basis.

Because it is abundant and relatively inefficient to ship (low value-to-weight ratio), coal is also generally consumed domestically by producing countries. For example, in 2006, only about 19 percent of global coal production was shipped overseas. Regional drivers should always be considered when evaluating coal producers.[15]

**Regional Versus Global** Global factors, however, can matter as some grades of coal with a high enough value are exported—steam (or thermal) coal and metallurgical (or coking) coal. Steam coal is used for power generation and metallurgical coal is used by steel producers (recall from Chapter 2, iron ore + coal = steel). Australia has been the largest coal exporter, with Japan, South Korea, and Taiwan—all lacking domestic resources—among the largest importers. The largest coal reserves belong to the US (27 percent), followed by Russia (17 percent), and then China (13 percent).[16] Because an export market does exist, firms will divert production to take advantage of higher prices if export market prices deviate enough from regional prices. The subsequent reduction in regional market supply will drive up regional prices until a balance is reached. Therefore, regional and global prices tend to rise together, although not necessarily in equal amounts as significant rail and port infrastructure can be required to export additional product (similar to iron ore). Therefore, the more coal a firm sells regionally, and the lower its access to developed rail and port systems, the more important regional drivers will be relative to global ones.

Note: Not all coal producers fall in the Materials sector. All of Materials' coal exposure is from diversified miners—who are some of the world's largest coal producers, but who also mine a variety of other metals. All pure coal producers fall within the Coal & Consumable Fuels sub-industry in the Energy sector. For more on how a pure coal producer fits within your portfolio's Energy allocation, refer to *Fisher Investments on Energy*. Additional coal information can also be found at the World Coal Institute (www.worldcoal.org) and the Energy Information Administration (www.eia.doe.gov).

## Steel

Steel is used in construction, transportation, manufacturing, and almost every segment of an economy. Demand tends to fluctuate with general economic growth, making the industry extremely cyclical.

Because steel comes in hundreds of grades and shapes serving specific markets and has a relatively low value-to-weight ratio, steel is priced, and should be evaluated, regionally. For example, in 2007, South Korea had by far the world's largest commercial shipbuilding industry, serving as a primary driver of the country's steel demand. By comparison, in the US, autos and non-residential construction were the largest end markets, and shipbuilding was only a fractional percentage.

Such regional end markets also caused the steel industry to become fragmented—in 2006, the top 15 steel producers only represented about one-third of global steel production.[17] Although it's priced regionally, like with coal, significant steel trade does take place. In 2007, the US imported about 25 percent of the steel it

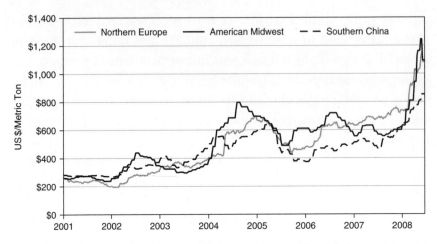

**Figure 4.2   Surveyed Hot-Rolled Coil Prices in US, Europe, and China**

*Source:* Bloomberg Finance L.P.

consumed.[18] As with coal, exporting steel reduces a region's supply and drives up regional prices until a balance is reached. Therefore, regional prices generally move in the same direction as global prices. You can see regional and global prices moving in the same direction, though in different magnitudes, in Figure 4.2. The graph shows prices of one of the most common types of steel for the US, Europe, and China. In the second half of 2003, China had the group's highest steel prices; but by the start of 2006, it had the lowest prices. Such fluctuations are due to regional events like changes in regional supply and demand, shipping rates, tariffs, and currency fluctuations.

**Bar Steel Versus Flat Steel** Of the hundreds of types and grades of steel, there are two major categories: *bar steel* (or long steel) and *flat steel*. Bar steel is almost exclusively used in construction, including re-bar, merchant bar, i-beams—most types of structural supports, rods, and wires. In the US, commercial construction consumes about 60 percent of bar steel, public infrastructure 30 percent, and residential construction a mere 10 percent.[19]

Flat steel is flat sheets, in many different grades, and can be shaped and used for everything—from autos to ships to machines. Hot-rolled steel—poured into flat sheets—is the most common. Cold-rolled—run through rollers to increase its density and change its strength and flexibility—is of higher value.

### Steel Alloys

Steel can be structurally modified or alloyed with other metals to change its characteristics. It can be hardened with the use of metals like molybdenum and vanadium, protected from rust with a zinc coating to form galvanized steel, or combined with nickel and chrome to form stainless steel. Galvanized steel is used where wear is not a concern—its rust resistance is compromised if the zinc coating is scratched. Stainless steel, however, retains its rust-proof resistance regardless of wear.

**Iron Ore Versus Scrap-Based Production** Steel producers can be segmented by their production process. Iron ore–based producers use basic oxygen furnaces, and scrap-based producers (called mini-mills) use electric arc furnaces. Most mini-mills are found in industrialized nations because they have access to more scrap from a longer industrialized history. In 2006, mini-mills represented 57 percent of steel production in the US and only 13 percent in China.[20]

As covered in Chapter 2, if scrap is abundant, mini-mills have a number of advantages over traditional iron ore–based producers, including lower energy and transportation costs.

**Vertical Integration** Vertical integration is important in this industry because processors are dependent on a steady stream of raw materials. Regional factors often determine the amount of vertical integration. Producers in iron ore–rich regions like Brazil, Russia, or Australia generally have more upstream vertical integration than producers in Japan or South Korea. Scrap-based producers can also be vertically integrated with upstream scrap sourcing and processing operations. When raw material prices are rising, self-sufficiency in iron ore, scrap steel processing, or coal is very advantageous. Higher raw material costs increase competitors' production costs, forcing them to raise prices. If prices rise industry-wide, but production costs don't change for a producer self-sufficient in raw materials, then that producer can experience higher margins and earnings. In the same environment, scrap processing is less advantageous than owning iron ore mines because scrap must continuously be sourced and purchased, whereas a mine's costs are relatively fixed. This trait cuts both ways. It's less advantageous to own upstream operations when raw material prices are falling.

Because they are priced regionally, most steel products are not exchange traded. However, in 2008 the LME began listing a few steel products for the first time. A futures curve showing price expectations for them can be found at their website (www.lme.co.uk/steel.asp). Additional steel information can be found at the International Iron & Steel Institute (www.worldsteel.org).

## Gold

Everyone's favorite shiny yellow metal has been used for centuries as a store of wealth, alternate currency, and adornment for men and women alike. Gold is highly valued, priced globally, and has captured the public's imagination like few other materials, attracting investors for centuries.

**Gold Consumption** Jewelry is the dominant end market for gold, with investor, industrial, and dental demand comprising the rest. Due to consumption of gold jewelry, India is gold's largest consumer. The country's massive rural population and limited historical banking infrastructure make gold jewelry one of the primary stores of value and a way of passing wealth between generations. In fact, it's so heavily used in Indian dowries that global gold demand typically sees a seasonal increase during India's wedding season.

Gold is relatively unique among the basic materials because investors can consume it directly, whereas most basic materials are consumed almost exclusively for industrial purposes. This makes gold

### Golden Baubles

Most of the world's gold jewelry is not set at a fixed price. Instead, it's sold primarily by weight and varies each day based on the international price, plus a small markup. Periods of high volatility can lead to a decline in global jewelry consumption as consumers refrain from buying, hesitant to find out later they could have bought it for a much lower price.

demand rather fickle—it can shift wildly with investor sentiment. Other precious metals like platinum and silver share this trait, but to a lesser degree. Investors typically demand gold as a store of value. When the risk of holding paper money is perceived to be increasing, gold's attractiveness increases.

Recall Figure 2.5 showed inflation increasing in the 1970s and the subsequent run-up in gold prices. Near its peak in 1980, investor demand had risen to 35 percent of total consumption. After the stable monetary periods of the 1980s and 1990s, however, investor demand for gold declined and gold prices stagnated. By 2000, it had dropped to just 4 percent of consumption. In 2007, investor fears of the US financial system and inflation from rising raw material prices along with the introduction of gold ETFs (exchange traded funds), stoked investor demand for gold once again. Investor consumption rose to account for 19 percent of consumption in 2007, and gold prices rose once again.[21]

### Gold ETF Popularity

Gold ETFs have become an increasingly popular way to gain gold exposure because the ETFs purchase and store the metal on your behalf—yet can be bought and sold on a daily basis like any other stock. The ability to track gold's price (minus fees) without having to arrange for shipment, storage, and locating buyers and sellers makes the investment far more liquid and attractive to investors.

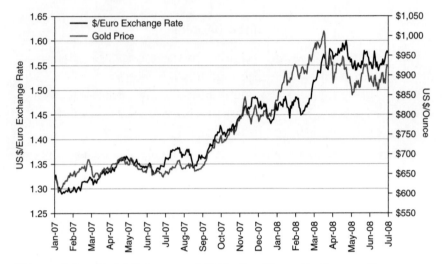

**Figure 4.3   Gold Prices vs. US Dollar/Euro Exchange Rate**
*Source:* Thomson Datastream.

Figure 4.3 shows how closely demand for gold can be tied to its role as a store of value. From the start of 2007 through mid-2008, a strong negative correlation existed between the strength of the US dollar and the price of gold. As the US dollar weakened and demand for an alternative store of value increased, gold prices correspondingly rose. Don't be fooled—the strength of this relationship can vary widely over time depending on investor sentiment, and a weak dollar is by no means a sign investors should always load up on gold.

Because gold is viewed by many as an alternate store of value, gold producers tend to have higher stock market valuations (P/Es, etc.) than most mining companies. Most metals' worth is defined by their usefulness since virtually all consumption of most metals is for industrial purposes. This can fluctuate significantly over time depending on the economic environment and available technology. As a store of value, however, gold's worth is perceived (rightly or wrongly) to be more stable with fewer risks to future substitution or replacement. Therefore, producers are generally expected to generate more stable cash flows.

**Gold Production** Beyond the normal capital-intensive barriers to entry for mining any material, gold's greatest barrier to entry is its scarcity. It's just not easy to locate in commercial quantities, and reserve replacement is a constant priority for producers. Changes in gold supply can affect prices and profitability just as much as demand. While gold prices rose during the 1970s on increased demand, supply was also falling—global production declined 15 percent. Conversely, from 1980 to 2000, improvements in refining technology, as well as the opening of new exploration areas in a more developed China and the former Soviet Union, led to a 110 percent increase in production—and gold prices struggled. From 2000 to 2007, prices again found their footing as demand increased and production declined 5 percent over the period.[22]

### Gold Bugs Should Bug You

Many believe gold is a good long-term store of wealth. By the end of 2007, however, gold had only returned 59 percent cumulatively since 1980, while the S&P 500 returned 1,260 percent. Which would you have rather owned?

*Source:* Thomson Datastream.

Another source of potential gold supply is central banks—in 2007, global central banks held roughly 30,000 tons of gold. Fortunately, central bankers understand their ability to impact the market and are usually very deliberate with their sales. (A detailed listing of central bank gold holdings can be found at the World Gold Council—www.research.gold.org/reserve_asset.)

Gold producers can also affect supply and demand in the futures market through *hedging* activity. Producers often sell future production for a set price today to protect against a decline in gold's value or to help fund new projects. To eliminate or cover their positions, they must purchase gold contracts.

**Future Prices** Gold is traded globally on futures exchanges, and future price expectations can be found at the New York Mercantile Exchange (NYMEX, available at www.nymex.com). Additional information can also be found at the World Gold Council (www.market-intelligence.gold.org).

## Aluminum

Though the aluminum sub-industry is relatively small, many diversified miners also derive significant earnings from the material. While the production process has improved over time, including a 40 percent improvement in energy efficiency over the last 50 years, an estimated 40 to 45 percent of its average production cost in 2007 was energy.[23] Therefore, the material is sometimes referred to by industry insiders as "solid energy."[24]

### The Joys of Recycling Aluminum

Recycling aluminum takes 95 percent less energy than producing it from scratch. Because energy is such a high percentage of total aluminum production costs, it is obvious why aluminum is one of the most commonly recycled metals on earth.

*Source:* The Aluminum Association.

Aluminum starts as bauxite, one of the most common ores in the earth's crust. Bauxite is mined, broken down in a chemical bath, and heated to create alumina, a white powder. Alumina is then dissolved into liquid form and undergoes an extremely energy-intensive process of electrolysis to create aluminum. Because aluminum processing is so costly, aluminum producers typically have higher variable costs than miners, and energy prices are extremely important in determining aluminum prices and producers' profitability.

When energy prices are low, producers may choose to focus on expanding in areas with low construction and capital costs. When energy prices are high, however, producers typically expand in regions with a competitive advantage in energy. From 2006 through 2008, as energy prices increased to record levels—with the exception of China and its partially subsidized producers—most new aluminum production was focused on low-cost power regions, including Iceland (geothermal), Brazil (hydroelectric), Canada (hydroelectric), and the Middle East (oil and natural gas).

Aluminum's largest end markets are transportation (airplanes and autos—more aluminum than steel is now used in autos), construction, and packaging. In 2007, these end markets combined to account for about 70 percent of aluminum's end use. A full breakdown of the metal's end use can be found through the LME (www.lme.co.uk/aluminium_industryusage.asp)—where you can also see future price expectations because aluminum is traded globally.

## Nickel

Nickel is currently less of an industry revenue driver than the other materials previously covered, fluctuating between being the fourth or fifth most important material depending on pricing and volumes. Therefore, it likely doesn't require as much of your analytical attention and we'll cover it in less detail.

Stainless steel is the primary end market for nickel and the primary driver of consumption growth. In 2007, stainless steel accounted for about two-thirds of consumption and virtually all of the consumption growth. Stainless steel's end markets are rather varied, with autos and construction being the largest components. Nickel is traded globally on futures exchanges, and future price expectations can be found through the LME (www.lme.co.uk/nickel.asp). Additional information on production and consumption can also be found through the LME (www.lme.co.uk/nickel_industryusage.asp) and the International Nickel Study Group (INSG, available at www.insg. org). Although some of the INSG's data is only available for a fee, the speaker presentations are free and often provide good summaries.

## Zinc

Zinc is an even smaller revenue driver than nickel. Galvanized steel has been its primary end market, followed by brass production—and don't forget: US pennies are 97.5 percent zinc, too! In 2007, galvanized steel consumed about 50 percent of production, and brass consumed about 20 percent. The primary demand drivers are construction and autos. More information on zinc, its uses, and regional production can be found through the LME (www.lme.co.uk/zinc_industryusage.asp). The International Lead & Zinc Study Group (www.ilzsg.org) is also a useful resource for learning more or following the metal in greater detail. Similar to the INSG, some of its data is available for a fee, but the presentations are free. Zinc is traded globally on futures exchanges, and future price expectations can be found through the LME (www.lme.co.uk/zinc.asp).

## CHEMICALS

In the previous chapter, we discussed why basic material prices are typically the most important Materials sector driver. While a good guideline, it's not always true for chemicals *because chemical production is not based on monetizing limited assets in the ground, but rather in processing abundant existing assets into something else.* Chemical producers' earnings are driven by production growth combined with prices, minus the cost of production.

With that in mind, let's look at Chemicals' major sub-industries more closely (Diversified Chemicals is excluded since it's a combination of Commodity and Specialty Chemical.):

1. Commodity Chemicals
2. Specialty Chemicals
3. Fertilizers & Agricultural Chemicals
4. Industrial Gases

### Commodity Chemicals

The most common commodity chemicals—ethylene and propylene—are priced globally and shipped in bulk. Their major end markets are specialty chemicals. However, some commodity chemicals are not used as widely and have more regional pricing characteristics.

No shortage of feedstock exists to produce commodity chemicals (chemical production only makes up a small percentage of total oil and natural gas consumption), so production is constrained only by profitability. Recall from Chapter 1 that firms compete primarily on prices. Therefore, competition to lower production costs is cutthroat in the battle for market share. The lack of pricing power also makes commodity chemical production extremely cyclical and dependent on economic growth.

An example of the importance of production costs can be seen in the expansion of commodity chemical production in the Middle East following the dramatic increase in energy prices from 2003 to 2008. Higher energy prices increased production costs and forced commodity chemical prices higher. This significantly increased earnings for any firm self-sufficient in the raw material. The Middle East took advantage of its dominant position in oil and natural gas by building enough large commodity chemical processing centers to double its ethylene capacity and increase global capacity by over 25 percent from 2006 through 2011.[25]

Only the largest commodity chemicals are exchange traded. Future prices of low density polyethylene and polypropylene (essentially ethylene and propylene) can be found through the LME (www.lme.co.uk/plastics.asp).

## Specialty Chemicals

Covering all specialty chemicals would turn this book into a multivolume encyclopedia, so instead we'll briefly highlight carbon fiber because of its growing importance. Remember: Specialty chemicals are typically priced regionally because they service regional and niche markets, often working closely with end customers to meet specific needs. This increases pricing power and reduces cyclicality relative to commodity chemicals. Also recall from Chapter 1 the analogy of the chemical production process as a tree. With thousands of branches, the only force powerful enough to push them all in the same direction at the same time is the broad tailwind of economic growth.

**Carbon Fiber** Carbon fiber has been around since at least the late 1800s. In fact, Thomas Edison used carbon fibers as filaments in some of his first light bulbs. High-strength carbon fibers weren't developed until the early 1960s and didn't emerge in commercial application until the 1970s. High-strength carbon fibers are thin strands of carbon-based fiber heated at high temperatures in the absence of oxygen. Without oxygen, the fiber can't burn and instead causes the fibers to vibrate and expel non-carbon atoms, creating a super strong chain of carbon. The material's extremely high strength-to-weight ratio makes it ideal for use in aerospace and autos, where lighter means faster and more fuel efficient.

Equipment and technology is by far the most costly component of production (carbon fibers themselves are made from petroleum). Until very recently, production costs kept carbon fiber out of widespread commercial use, though that didn't stop the military from developing jet fighters with it. Recent improvements in technology over the last decade, however, dramatically dropped production costs and opened a new array of uses. Today, lower-grade carbon fiber is commonly used in sports equipment, industrial applications, and turbines (propellers in wind farms). High-grade carbon fiber is used in new commercial aerospace designs (approximately 50 percent of Boeing's new 787 plane and 25 percent of the structure of Airbus' new A380 is made from carbon fiber).[26] Aerospace is the largest end market for carbon fiber—in 2006, an estimated 40 percent of total carbon fiber demand was from aerospace. A detailed breakdown of its end uses can be found through Zoltek, one of the few US-based carbon fiber producers (www.zoltek.com/carbonfiber/future.php).Carbon fiber is also being tested in cars, but is primarily used so far in Formula One race cars and other high-end applications where cost is less of a consideration. However, the higher the price of fuel, the more attractive carbon fiber becomes for autos. Should oil prices rise high enough and carbon fiber's production costs continue to fall, you could one day drive a very light and fuel-efficient car whose structure contains virtually no metal at all.

Because of significant technological barriers, barriers to entry are high. And because of its military applications, the technology behind producing high-grade carbon fiber in particular is closely guarded by governments. This has led to a concentrated industry and high operating margins. In 2007, operating margins averaged over 20 percent and only seven major producers existed, with three of them (Toray, Teijin, and Mitsubishi Rayon—all Japan-based) controlling 70 percent of the market.[27] Carbon fiber is priced regionally and by its specific grade and end market. Therefore, it's not priced on a futures exchange, and future price expectations are not easily determined. Future production and consumption forecasts, however, are obtainable through industry trade sources such as Composites World (www.compositesworld.com).

### Commoditization of New Technologies

New technologies often start with high barriers to entry and producers are rewarded with higher valuations. Over time, however, the technology typically spreads, causing the product to become increasingly commoditized. As this happens, producer valuations often decline.

## Fertilizers & Agricultural Chemicals

Fertilizers & Agricultural Chemicals includes fertilizers, pesticides, herbicides, fungicides, and genetically modified seed producers. Demand is primarily driven by changes in food consumption, the corresponding adjustment in food production, and advancements in farming technology. Some of the largest potential food consumption drivers include population growth, increased consumption of meat, and increased consumption of biofuels. Meat consumption can significantly impact crop demand. Why? It takes about two kilograms of feed to produce one kilogram of chicken, four kilograms of feed to produce one kilogram of pork, and seven kilograms of feed to produce one kilogram of beef.[28]

### No Vegetarians Here

The greatest potential for changing consumption patterns comes from rising wealth in emerging markets, but patterns can change in the developed world as well. A 2005 study by the USDA found the average American eats 200 pounds of meat a year, a 22-pound-per-person increase since 1970.

*Source:* US Department of Agriculture.

Government regulations also have significant impacts through tariffs, subsidies, and bio-fuel mandates. Driven by government mandates, US corn-based ethanol capacity doubled from 2001 to 2005 and doubled again by the end of 2008.[29] Production was also encouraged by a $0.51 per gallon subsidy and $0.54 per gallon tariff on otherwise cheaper sugarcane-based imports from Brazil. The growth in ethanol consumption has significantly impacted crop demand. Ethanol processing consumed 14 percent of the US corn crop in 2005 and 25 percent in 2008.[30]

Due to increased meat consumption and growth in bio-fuels, food demand is projected to increase between 2.5 to 3.5 times by 2050 despite the population increasing by less than 50 percent.[31] This sub-industry, however, should not be expected to provide all of the necessary growth in crop production. Better farming methods, more efficient equipment, better distribution networks, and improved technology (like refrigeration) will also increase the availability and supply of food. In 2006, poor infrastructure and a lack of refrigeration meant over 30 percent of all produce in India spoiled before reaching the consumer[32]—a little technology would go a long way toward increasing food supply in many regions.

**Genetically Modified Seeds & Crop Chemicals** Genetically modified seed producers often look more like technology companies with patents and proprietary technology, separating producers and serving as a barrier to entry for competitors. The barriers are high, so only a handful of producers exist. Nonetheless, they're still beholden to the sub-industry's fundamental drivers. Genetically modified seed producers are tackling the same problems as crop chemicals like pesticides and fungicides—preventing damage from pests and fungi—so most firms involved in one are also involved in the other. Seed producers breed resistance into the plant, and crop chemical producers attack the problem externally. Even herbicides cross over, with genetically modified seed producers breeding in resistance to strong herbicides capable of killing all other plants. This reduces the need to crop dust with multiple types of specialized and expensive weed killers, designed to only kill certain families of plants.

Prices are set regionally. Governments are often involved in regulating producers because there are social fears of genetically modified food in many countries. Despite the fears, emerging market countries have been quick to (rather sensibly) accept genetically modified crops because of potential yield gains. In 2007, global planting of genetically modified crops increased 12 percent, with a 21 percent growth rate in emerging markets, but only a 6 percent growth rate in the developed world.[33] It is easy to see why emerging markets have embraced the technology. In 2002, India introduced genetically modified cotton capable of resisting a pesky caterpillar called the bollworm. By 2007, it had gone from being a net importer of cotton to the world's third largest exporter, and total production roughly doubled.[34]

Emerging markets aren't alone in implementing the technology. The US has also generally been quick to accept it. In 2008, more than 70 percent of the US corn crop was genetically modified.[35] Europe has consistently been the slowest to accept such crops due to social opposition.

**Fertilizers** One of the easiest and least controversial ways to increase crop yields is through fertilizer use. Manufactured fertilizer in particular can have a tremendous influence on yields, with one pound of chemical fertilizer holding the equivalent nutrients of over 40 pounds of fresh manure.[36] Fertilizer has three key ingredients: *nitrogen, phosphate,* and *potash.*

### Why Starvation Persists in the Twenty-First Century

Starvation does not occur because of a lack of food globally, but because of lacking infrastructure, high trade barriers, limited property rights, or excessive government intervention. To quote the World Bank's 2003 World Development Report, "The prevailing view of agricultural economists is that the world food problem is one of insufficient purchasing power in the hands of poor people, not of global constraints on aggregate food production—even with an expanded population."

*Source:* The World Bank and Oxford University Press, "Sustainable Development in a Dynamic World," World Development Report 2003, pp. 84–85.

Nitrogen is manufactured and priced regionally. It's processed from natural gas in manufacturing plants and commonly concentrated into ammonia or urea. Phosphate and potash, however, are mined out of the ground and shipped around the world. Following iron ore, coal, and grains, more fertilizer is shipped globally than any other dry good. While phosphate production has been relatively evenly distributed, potash (sourced from large old marine deposits) is scarce, so production is very concentrated. In 2006, about 70 percent of phosphate production came from large and diverse regions of Africa, the US, and China, while nearly 70 percent of potash production came from just a few areas in Canada, Russia, and Belarus. Many of the same constraints and barriers to entry that apply to metal miners also apply to fertilizer miners. This includes extremely capital-intensive operations and long lead times of 5 to 10 years to develop a new mine.[37]

## Industrial Gases

The Industrial Gas sub-industry is a relatively small component of most benchmarks and not currently vital to driving sector returns. It's distinct enough, however, to be worth briefly covering. The Industrial

Gas sub-industry produces everything from small canisters of helium for local party balloon stores to massive pipelines of hydrogen for oil refineries. Other commonly produced gases include nitrogen, oxygen, and argon. On a basic level, the primary use for industrial gases is to create or prevent chemical reactions. This is primarily useful during the formation of other materials. In 2007, at about a third of total consumption, the chemical and refining industry was the largest end market for industrial gases, followed by metal production and electronics manufacturing.[38] With these end markets, economic growth, energy expenditures, and industrial manufacturing are all key drivers.

Industrial gas is delivered to customers in either small cylinders (packaged gases—used for retail use or expensive specialty gases that make the cost of shipping small quantities more feasible), bulk liquid tankers (merchant gases), or via direct pipelines (tonnage gases) from onsite production facilities. The products are inefficient to ship long distances so they are priced regionally. Even when compressed under pressure, it's relatively uneconomical to ship a canister very far. The most economic means of shipping gas is to condense it to a liquid. Unfortunately for this industry, once liquefied, its gases are no longer economical to ship long distances on a value-to-weight ratio. Therefore, the industry primarily operates on a regional basis. While different gases are produced in different ways, most industrial gas is produced by using energy to separate components from air, water, or natural gas. Therefore, energy and natural gas in particular serve as the primary variable costs. Depending on the firm, transportation and fuel costs can also be important.

### Gas at Work

Oil refineries are the largest single users of industrial gas, using over 12 billion cubic feet of hydrogen per day. This works out to an average of 100 to 200 cubic feet of hydrogen to process one barrel of oil. Oil drillers also use tremendous amounts of carbon dioxide, which is pumped into wells to pressure oil to the surface.

*Source:* QuestAir, "Hydrogen for Oil Refining."

## CONSTRUCTION MATERIALS

Construction materials are priced regionally and the industry should be evaluated regionally. This is especially true of construction aggregate—one of the least efficient materials to ship. Regional events play a dominant role in demand for most producers. Outside of normal regional construction trends, three of the largest world events providing regional demand for construction materials are World Cups, Olympics, and World's Fairs.

You can see the divergent regional trends by comparing the US to emerging markets from 2006 through 2008. A lack of new quarry approvals made construction aggregate supply limited in the US, but quarries were abundant in emerging markets, creating very different pricing trends. Prices in the US rose, despite a steep decline in sales volumes tied to the US housing downturn. Prices in many regions of emerging markets, however, were relatively stagnant or even declined, despite large increases in sales volumes tied to infrastructure build outs. The primary driver for construction materials, including concrete, cement, and construction aggregate, is construction activity. Two-thirds of total US cement consumption occurs during the summer building period of May to October.[39] Figure 4.4 shows total construction spending in the US relative to the performance of the Construction Materials industry. Notice how the industry grew with total construction during the housing boom, and then fell once construction declined.

Total construction is the primary driver for all products in this industry. Construction aggregate is more sensitive to non-residential construction because it's heavily used in road building. Cement is slightly more sensitive to residential construction.

Additional information for the US market, including annual cement production and consumption on a state by state basis, can be found at the Portland Cement Association (www.cement.org/econ/index.asp).

## PAPER & FOREST PRODUCTS

Paper & Forest Products are a very small portion of the Materials sector in most benchmarks, so we'll cover it only briefly. The products in

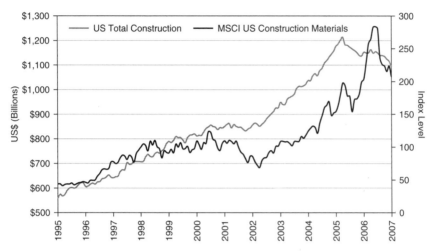

**Figure 4.4    Total US Construction vs. MSCI US Construction Materials**

Source: Thomson Datastream; MSCI Inc.[40]

this industry are priced regionally and producers should be evaluated on a regional basis.

## Paper Products

Because of its use in periodicals, consumer goods, shipping, and general office activity, paper and paperboard demand is economically sensitive. Although some forecasted a significant decline in paper consumption during the 1990s technology revolution, consumption has not drastically declined (outside of newsprint). In fact, global consumption of paper and paperboard increased 40 percent from 1993 to 2004.[41] The largest end markets are printing and writing paper, containerboard, and boxboard—in 2000, they combined to form 80 percent of US consumption.[42] Unlike much of this sector, where emerging markets play such a central role in supply and demand, the developed world is the primary consumer and producer of paper products. Based on wood pulp consumption, North America, Western Europe, and Japan combined to produce nearly 70 percent of the world's paper in 2007.[43]

## Forest Products

Forest Products (i.e., lumber) are priced regionally, though some overseas trade does exist in hardwoods with higher value-to-weight ratios. But softwoods are rarely shipped long distances in significant quantities.

The primary driver for lumber is residential construction—the numbers shift from year to year, but it's not unusual for new home starts to account for up to 40 percent of US consumption.[44] Although significant overseas trade of lumber and softwood in particular is rare, the US is the largest importer of forestry products in the world. The reason is its proximity to Canada—which has about 10 percent of the world's total forests.[45]

Environmental and regulatory factors often play a large role in this industry, including the Endangered Species Act of 1973 and the Roadless Area Conservation Rule in 2001. In 1990, the Endangered Species Act protected 6.9 million acres of federal timber land in the Pacific Northwest—an area larger than the states of Massachusetts and Rhode Island combined—for the spotted owl.[46] The Roadless Area Conservation Rule of 2001 protected about a third of the national forest system's total acreage, or 58 million acres, from roads and logging.[47]

In Europe, Sweden and Finland have historically been the largest net exporters of paper and forestry products.[48] After the fall of the Soviet Union, however, Russia began to emerge as the dominant regional force—its vast natural resources and investments in the paper and sawmill industries had long been neglected under communist rule. Russia has the largest timber reserves in Europe, with an estimated one-fifth of the world's softwood forests and has become one of the world's largest lumber producers.

## CONTAINERS & PACKAGING

We've largely ignored containers and packaging so far. It's such a tiny part of the sector that you really don't need to worry about it. The industry is generally considered to be defensive, with relatively inelastic demand through economic cycles. In other words, demand for this industry's products remains about the same in good times and bad. The main reason is because the largest segment of the industry is food and beverages. For example, in 2003, an estimated 40 percent of containers were used for packaging food and 20 percent for beverages.[49] One of the industry's most important drivers is its production costs, so many packaging firms have relocated manufacturing plants to emerging market countries with cheaper operating environments. High oil and natural gas prices are also a negative because they're heavily used to produce two of the industries' largest segments, plastic bottles and aluminum cans. Updated news on the industry can be found at Packaging Today (www.packagingtoday.com). Given the amount of paper used in packaging, this site also often has useful updates on the Paper & Forest Products industry.

## Chapter Recap

You should now be familiar with each industry in the Materials sector, its most important components, and its drivers. However, drivers change in importance and relevance over time, so remain vigilant.

Ultimately, supply and demand determine pricing for basic materials, and there's no silver bullet or rule of thumb that works every time to determine future pricing, earnings, or stock performance. Instead, careful analysis is required to determine what's most important at any given time and to predict whether an industry will be more or less profitable than the market expects.

- The Materials sector is value-oriented and extremely concentrated into a small group of dominant firms.
- Iron ore—priced globally on annual contracts. Infrastructure is as important as mines in determining production. This creates high barriers to entry, the need for economies of scale, and a concentrated group of producers.
- Coal—primarily priced regionally on annual contracts, but a global export market does exist. Steam coal (for energy) and metallurgical coal (for steel production) are priced differently.

*(Continued)*

- Steel—priced regionally with key distinctions among producers: bar versus flat steel production, and scrap-based mini-mills versus traditional iron ore–based operations. Significant trade and exports for many products exist as well.
- Gold—priced globally with the relatively unique trait of having investors as an end market. Scarcity is its primary barrier to entry.
- Aluminum—priced globally and by far the most energy-intensive metal. Energy costs are the primary determinant of price and returns.
- Commodity Chemicals—priced globally with economic growth as its primary driver, and oil and natural gas as its primary input cost.
- Specialty Chemicals—most are priced regionally. Economic growth and specific end markets for each segment are the drivers.
- Fertilizers & Agricultural Chemicals—priced regionally for most products. Demand for increased crop production through greater yields is the primary driver.
- Industrial Gases—priced regionally with natural gas as a primary input cost. Economic growth, industrial manufacturing, metal and chemical production, and oil refining are primary drivers.
- Construction Materials—priced regionally and dependent on construction as its primary driver. Construction aggregate in particular sees very little trade and is extremely regional in nature. Cement is more sensitive to residential construction, while construction aggregate is more sensitive to non-residential construction.
- Paper & Forestry—primarily priced regionally with residential construction as the primary driver for lumber, while economic growth is the primary driver for paper. Environmental legislation can play a big role.
- Packaging—primarily a defensive sector with relatively inelastic demand due to food and beverage being its largest components.

# 5

# STAYING CURRENT

## Tracking Sector Fundamentals

By now, you should have an understanding of the Materials sector's history, structure, and drivers. But how do you keep track of the sector moving forward?

There are really only three items to track:

1. Supply
2. Demand
3. Sentiment

Higher demand for a static supply level supports higher prices and higher earnings. And regardless of earnings growth, sentiment can get overheated, causing firms to become overvalued in what can become a bubble (though actual bubbles are far rarer than most think). Or it can cause firms to become undervalued, which often happens near the bottom of a bear market and sometimes in bull market corrections. But to understand if a firm is under- or overvalued, you must understand how to track the direction of high-level drivers and fundamentals.

## Using Industry Concentration to Your Advantage

You needn't track every Materials firm in the world to keep tabs on the factors impacting industries and sub-industries. Tracking the largest and most dominant firms often provides insight on important near-term factors impacting the entire industry (see Table 4.6 for industry concentrations). Quarterly earnings presentations (on company websites), conference calls, and analyst Q&A at the end of conference calls are often good sources (conference call transcripts can be found at http://seekingalpha.com/tag/transcripts). The 10 largest firms in each Materials industry in the MSCI All Country World Index (one of the broadest indexes) are listed in Appendix B.

## WHAT TO WATCH

It's not possible to list every potential factor affecting Materials. Instead, we'll focus on the most important and widely tracked fundamentals in determining supply and demand. Factors affecting globally priced materials should be tracked globally; likewise, factors affecting regionally priced goods should be tracked regionally. A list of industry data sources is also provided in Appendix A to help you perform your own research and analysis.

Fundamentals to watch include:

- Gross domestic product (GDP) growth
  - ◆ Residential and non-residential construction
  - ◆ Durable goods orders
  - ◆ Industrial production
- Global materials production growth
- Inventories
- Global materials trade (imports and exports)
- Capacity utilization
- Raw material costs
- Marginal cost of production
- Tariffs, royalties, subsidies, and price caps
- Freight rates

## Table 5.1    Bullish and Bearish Fundamentals for Prices of Basic Materials

| Bullish Drivers | Bearish Drivers |
| --- | --- |
| Rising GDP growth | Falling GDP growth |
| Rising non-residential construction | Falling non-residential construction |
| Rising residential construction | Falling residential construction |
| Rising durable goods orders | Falling durable goods orders |
| Rising industrial production | Falling industrial production |
| Falling global materials production | Rising global materials production |
| Falling inventories | Rising inventories |
| Rising global imports | Falling global imports (unless supply driven) |
| Rising capacity utilization | Falling capacity utilization |
| Rising raw material costs | Falling raw material costs |
| Rising marginal cost of production | Falling marginal cost of production |
| Increased commodity regulation (tariffs, etc.) | Decreased commodity regulation |
| Increased freight rates | Decreased freight rates |

Table 5.1 breaks these factors into bullish drivers—those likely to help drive the prices of basic materials higher—and bearish drivers.

### GDP Growth

Global GDP growth is the most powerful Materials demand driver (covered in Chapters 1 and 3). Rising global GDP per capita signals increasing industrialization as governments invest in infrastructure, causing productivity and standards of living to increase. Industrialized societies with high GDPs per capita consume more basic materials per capita (covered in Chapter 3). It's vital to shape an opinion on whether economic growth rates globally will be above or below expectations when making Materials sector decisions for your portfolio.

Gross domestic product (GDP) is also one of the easiest factors to track (but not necessarily to forecast, as any economist will attest). Detailed breakdowns of US GDP can be found through the US Bureau of Economic Analysis (www.bea.gov). Breakdowns of global GDP are at the International Monetary Fund (IMF, available at

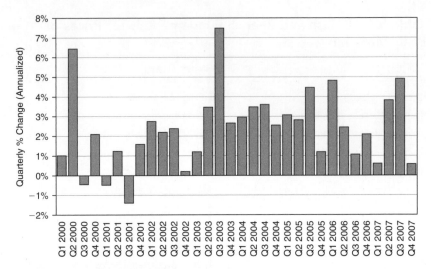

**Figure 5.1    US Real GDP by Quarter**
Source: Thomson Datastream.

www.imf.org). Both global and regional GDP are useful in tracking Materials consumption.

Remember GDP growth is often volatile and you should focus on the overall trend rather than getting caught up with any single quarter. This can be seen in Figure 5.1, which shows US quarterly GDP growth from 2000–2007. GDP growth varies widely and rarely forms a smooth line.

There are also a few economic components within GDP that Materials analysts pay especially close attention to involving construction and industrial output.

**Residential and Non-Residential Construction**    Residential and non-residential construction are major basic material consumers. These metrics are especially important for many regionally priced materials like steel, lumber, cement, construction aggregate, and some specialty chemicals, which are all heavily used construction materials. Less construction takes place during the winter, so it's important to compare this metric year over year.

As outlined in Chapter 4, bar steel is particularly sensitive to non-residential construction, lumber and some specialty chemicals

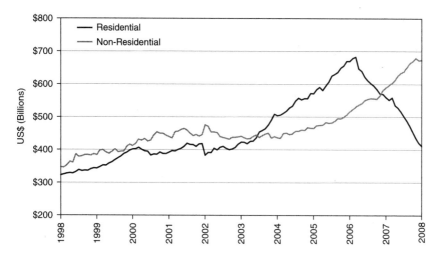

**Figure 5.2    US Residential and Non-Residential Construction Spending**

Source: Thomson Datastream.

are sensitive to residential construction, and cement and construction aggregate are sensitive to total construction. Figure 5.2 shows US residential and non-residential construction from 1998 through 2007. Bar steel provided strong results through the end of 2007. Lumber producers suffered when residential construction declined, as did paint producers, although more modestly because of less extreme exposure to residential construction (autos and consumer goods are also large end markets). Finally, cement and construction aggregate producers suffered once total construction began declining. In the US, these figures are released monthly by the US Census Bureau (www.census.gov).

**Durable Goods Orders**    Durable goods are produced to last longer than three years—cars, airplanes, or washing machines are durable goods, but shoes and shirts are not. Durable goods often make heavy use of basic materials, especially metals and plastics.

The US durable goods orders report is released monthly by the US Census Bureau. The reports are broken down by industry. The transportation industry is often removed from the report for more consistently comparable numbers because of the volatility involved in big ticket orders like airplanes. As you review this report, keep in mind that orders can be canceled.

**Industrial Production**    Industrial production is a measure of the total output of factories and mines and includes durable and nondurable goods. This is a more reliable measure of what is actually being produced, rather than just ordered. However, it's also backward-looking, while the durable goods orders report is forward-looking (i.e., predictive).

This useful metric in determining trends in US Materials consumption is released monthly by the Federal Reserve Board.

## Global Materials Production Growth

Global production growth in materials can dramatically impact prices by increasing supply. But for purposes of investing in stocks, it's always production *relative* to expectations rather than absolute production that matters. If global production increases but remains below expectations, basic materials prices will remain higher than anticipated, which lead to higher than anticipated earnings and usually rising stock prices. Given the long lead times (typically two years or more) in constructing highly capital-intensive production facilities, new production capacity for most of the sector can be predicted well in advance. Annual production forecasts are found through most trade publications or websites. (A list of these resources can be found in Appendix A.)

Despite the transparency into future production capacity, analysts routinely struggle to predict production. This is usually due to production disruptions like strikes, infrastructure bottlenecks, equipment failures, and weather-related outages like floods and hurricanes. When a firm can no longer fulfill its contracts, it declares *force majeure*. This invokes a standard contract clause that eliminates its liability for delivery failures. The clause only applies to events considered outside of the firm's control (e.g., hurricanes, floods), not negligence or malfeasance.

## Inventories

Global inventory levels are looked at closely as an indicator for consumption versus production, particularly for metals and commodity chemicals. Distributor inventory levels can be tracked to provide information about trends in consumption relative to production. However, products like specialty chemicals and construction aggregate serving regional or niche end markets typically sell directly to the end user and a consolidated traceable inventory often doesn't exist.

For goods priced globally on exchanges, analysts usually track only a few key global storage center networks. For goods priced regionally, analysis of each region's inventory levels (if available) is necessary to determine its impact. The most commonly tracked global inventories for industrial metals are at the LME. But steel inventories are tracked regionally through steel service center inventories (steel distributor warehouses).

Figure 5.3 shows LME copper inventory levels relative to price. As inventory levels declined and consumption increased faster than production, prices generally rose. Note that inventories are not a perfect indicator predicting every price movement. Instead, they can be used as a general guide.

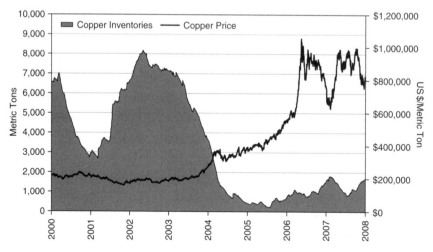

**Figure 5.3    Copper Prices vs. Inventories**
*Source:* Thomson Datastream.

## All Inventories Are Not Created Equal

Analysts track inventories in China, but China's inventories can mislead. The political environment is far from open, and estimating real inventory levels can be tricky. In the second half of 2006, copper prices confused many observers, causing some to predict a global economic downturn as prices fell by over 30 percent from early July through the following January. Global economic growth, however, remained strong, and copper prices eventually rebounded sharply in early 2007.

In hindsight, analysts suspect China built up inventories and stopped buying significant quantities of copper on the open market. Copper prices fell until China used its inventory and began repurchasing copper on the open market. Because of such distortions, inventories at the LME are generally considered more important. This also serves as an example why timing short-term moves can be fraught with danger.

*Source:* Bloomberg Finance L.P.

## Global Materials Trade: Imports and Exports

Changes in imports and exports provide an indication of changes in consumption and production. Since basic materials are among the most traded goods in the world (iron ore, coal, grains, and fertilizers make up the largest volumes of dry goods shipped globally),[1] tremendous trade data exists.

Fortunately, you needn't look at every country. Just focus on the main consumers and producers. China was the primary country responsible for the increased consumption of globally priced metals from 2000 to 2007, so it was important to track its imports during that period. (We'll explore China's Materials demand further in Chapter 6.)

Figure 5.4 shows China's copper imports from 2000 through 2007. China's monthly imports more than doubled over the period. Also notice how volatile imports can be, underscoring the importance of remaining focused on long-term trends. A decrease in global imports with no change in production usually means global demand is slowing, and prices will fall. Conversely, rising global imports signal

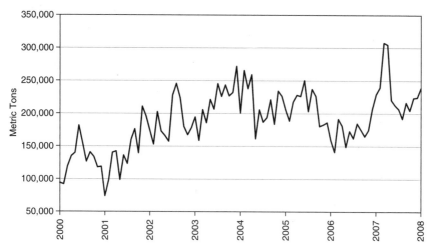

**Figure 5.4  China's Copper Imports 2000–2007**
*Source:* Thomson Datastream.

increased demand. If global production can't keep up and inventories simultaneously decline, prices will likely rise.

In some cases, falling global imports can be good for many producers, as long as it's driven by a shortfall in another producer's or region's supply rather than reduced demand. The numbers alone won't tell you which is happening, so if you see falling imports, you'll need to analyze why before determining if it's a positive or negative for most producers. For example, in early 2008, a large snowstorm in China caused widespread power outages and led to a significant reduction in aluminum production. The decline in production caused global aluminum prices to increase, benefiting all the producers outside of China.

For products like steel and aluminum with wide varieties of shapes and qualities, it's important to track net imports (imports minus exports) and net exports rather than just the absolute number. A country may simultaneously export and import large quantities of different grades of material, but we're most interested in the net effect. Exports and imports are among the most indicative reflections of global supply and demand.

## Capacity Utilization

*Capacity utilization* indicates the percentage of a region's or the world's production capacity currently being used. It's a useful proxy for measuring regional or global demand relative to the industries' potential production capabilities. For practical reasons (including maintenance and repair), capacity utilization will almost never reach 100 percent. In fact, anything over 90 percent is generally considered a very strong number and indicative of tight supplies relative to demand.

Capacity utilization usually rises in periods of high demand as firms increase production and maximize their production. In times of low demand, some facilities may be unprofitable to run and may sit idle or temporarily close for maintenance.

Not only are changes in capacity utilization closely watched to measure demand, it's also watched as an indicator of how quickly supply can increase. At a capacity utilization rate of 50 percent, an industry could dramatically increase production in a very short time to meet higher demand. With a capacity utilization rate of 95 percent, new production facilities are needed to meet new demand. In

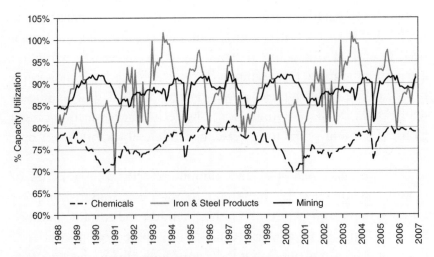

**Figure 5.5   Capacity Utilization of US Steel, Mining, and Chemicals**
Source: Thomson Datastream.

the Materials sector in particular (characterized by large and highly capital intensive projects) this can take years.

Figure 5.5 shows the capacity utilization rate of US steel, mining, and chemical industries from 1998 through 2007. Notice the utilization rate for some industries is more volatile than others because of maintenance needs and the greater ease with which production can be started and stopped. Note, too, capacity is simply an estimate made by the government and may not accurately reflect an industry's true capacity. This is why it's possible for capacity utilization to exceed 100 percent in some cases, as the US steel industry did in 1994 and 2004. The utilization rate is simply designed to give a rough estimate of current total capacity. The US capacity utilization figures are released monthly by the Federal Reserve.

## Raw Material Costs

Raw materials affect production costs and, therefore, profitability. Higher input costs force producers to pass costs on to consumers in the form of higher prices. In fragmented industries with limited pricing power, raw materials costs can greatly influence earnings and performance. Changing input costs have the greatest affect on chemicals, steel, paper, cement, and packaging since they are manufactured from a substrate material and have higher variable costs.

When raw material costs change dramatically, performance between vertically integrated producers (who produce their own raw materials) and non-vertically integrated producers can deviate widely (as covered in Chapter 4). Vertically integrated producers typically benefit when raw material costs are rising, but trail peers when costs decline.

## Marginal Cost of Production

The marginal cost of production is the cost of producing one additional unit of something. For any level of production, the price must remain above the cost of producing it, otherwise a company has no incentive to make additional products. In a perfectly competitive environment where supply can easily adjust, prices should remain at the marginal cost of production as firms increase production at any expense as long as it's profitable.

Industries with high barriers to entry, however, may see prices significantly exceed the marginal cost of production. When prices rise, firms have an incentive to increase production, but barriers prevent immediate new production (e.g., long lead times to develop a mine). This can magnify pricing responses to changes in demand.

An industry's cost of production can be represented by a cost curve where the average cost of every producer, country, or even individual mine is plotted. Figure 5.6 demonstrates a hypothetical example of a copper cost curve. Some producers have lower costs than others. Typically, the steeper the right end of the curve, the more constrained new production is as producers are forced into high cost production to bring additional product to the market. For our purposes the actual costs are less important than the shape of the curve. In recent years, copper's cost curve has risen steeply at the far right, indicating producers have struggled to find new low-cost production.

Costs are often represented net of byproducts to simplify the comparison between producers. If a copper mine also produces gold, the

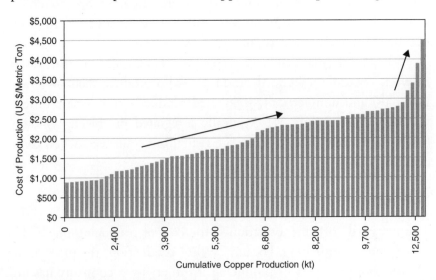

**Figure 5.6  Theoretical Copper Cost Curve**

revenue from the gold is offset against the cost of production, and a simpler calculation of its cost per pound of copper is calculated. This allows for a simple comparison across producers.

If prices are at the marginal cost of production and any factor causes marginal production costs to increase while desired consumption remains the same, prices will increase to ensure the desired production is profitable. If a producer or industry segment is unaffected by the increased costs, it will see margin expansion as prices rise and its costs remain the same.

## Tariffs, Royalties, Subsidies, and Price Caps

Changes in government tariffs (export and import taxes), royalties, subsidies, and price caps can dramatically impact regional and global prices. Although increased regulation is typically a negative for long-term economic growth due to the creation of irrational incentive structures, regulation can cause the prices of some goods to rise, especially in the short term. Because government intervention is not typically coordinated around the globe, it generally has greatest impact on local producers. If the country or region, however, is a large enough consumer or producer of a good, it can affect global supply and demand. Therefore, it's especially important to track government policies of the largest basic material consumers and producers. There's no centralized database of easily digestible information on this subject since there are thousands of countries, goods, and varying details of each regulation. But the World Trade Organization (WTO) is often a good resource. Government intervention and political sentiment is fickle and difficult to predict. In Chapter 6, we'll cover a number of examples on how regulations historically affect producers and industries.

## Freight Rates

Freight rates are the cost of shipping goods from one region to another and significantly impact regionally priced materials. As shipping costs rise, regional price differences can be expected to increase.

**Figure 5.7    Baltic Dry Index**
Source: Bloomberg Finance L.P.

Figure 5.7 shows the Baltic Dry Index—a widely tracked gauge for the cost of shipping dry goods in bulk (primarily raw materials)—from 1998 through 2007. Notice near the end of 2007, the index reached record levels because of high demand and rising fuel costs. This increased regional pricing disparity of basic materials around the world. It even caused 2008 annual iron ore contracts (typically priced globally) to include regional price differences based on freight charges. Due to their proximity and therefore lower freight rates, Australian iron ore producers were able to charge China, the world's largest iron ore consumer, a higher price than Brazilian producers.

## Chapter Recap

Fundamentals change over time and no single metric is always the most important or relevant when analyzing Materials prices. The dominant themes of supply, demand, and sentiment, however, remain throughout time as driving forces, and will always be important to track. It is also important to remain focused on long-term trends and not become overly sensitive to inherent short-term fluctuations in data.

- Economic growth is one of the most important drivers for basic material demand and can be tracked through government reports.

- Construction, industrial production, and durable goods orders are all subsets of economic growth. These are intensive in their use of basic materials and therefore require close scrutiny.
- Tracking production growth helps measure and forecast supply.
- Inventory levels provide an indication of trends in production versus consumption. Rising inventories indicate supply is gaining faster than demand, and prices can be expected to weaken over time. Falling inventories imply demand is gaining faster than supply, typically causing prices to rise over time.
- Import and export data provide insight into global trade, consumption, and production. Along with inventory changes, net imports, and net exports, reports from the largest producers and consumers of basic materials are often the first indication of changing global consumption or production patterns.
- Capacity utilization provide an indication of demand. The lower the capacity utilization, the more easily production can increase to meet new demand. The higher the capacity utilization, the less available additional production will be until new production facilities can be built.
- Raw material input costs affect profitability and therefore stock prices.
- The marginal cost of production determines the minimum price level for a determined consumption level and helps forecast prices. A cost curve quantifies the effects of barriers to entry.
- Tariffs, royalties, subsidies, and price caps are all forms of government intervention. They primarily affect producers on a regional basis since governments rarely coordinate such efforts. The effects can be difficult to predict, but may have significant consequences.
- Freight rates affect regional pricing disparities. The higher the rates, the less efficient it becomes to ship materials and the greater the regional pricing variations.

# CASE STUDY

## The 2003 to 2007
## Bull Market in Materials

**N**ow we can see the previously covered drivers at work by examining the Materials bull market from 2003 through 2007, focusing particularly on metals.

Today, emerging market countries are some of the primary basic materials consumers, and of metals in particular. In 2007, they consumed over 50 percent of global copper and iron ore production.[1] This wasn't always the case. The developed world was the dominant consumer and growth driver for many years. This changed over time as emerging markets began to industrialize. When the emerging markets' growth rate and industrialization process rapidly accelerated, its consumption of basic materials also began to dramatically impact global materials demand.

Emerging markets weren't the only consumption drivers during this period. Another structural change was the rebuild of aging developed market infrastructure. Much of the developed world was industrialized over 100 years ago. Pipes, bridges, roads, dams, and other

### Table 6.1    Metal Prices 2003 to 2007

| Metal | (%) Return 12/31/02–12/31/07 |
|---|---|
| Copper | 337 |
| Nickel | 272 |
| Zinc | 218 |
| Silver | 216 |
| Iron Ore* | 189 |
| Platinum | 156 |
| Gold | 144 |
| Steel** | 94 |
| Aluminum | 77 |

*Source:* Thomson Datastream; International Monetary Fund.

\* Iron ore fines, 67.55% iron content (FOB)

\*\* US Imports Hot Rolled Coil Steel (FOB)

infrastructures showed increasing deterioration and in some cases began to fail, requiring significant repairs.

The impact of these events on the Materials sector, and Metals & Mining in particular, was notable. The Metals & Mining industry of the MSCI All Country World Index provided a cumulative negative 12 percent return from 1995 through 2002, but a 468 percent return from 2003 through 2007.

The cause of the dramatic stock performance can be seen in Table 6.1. The tremendous increase in basic materials prices led to higher earnings, driving stock prices higher. Of course, demand doesn't tell the whole story. Prices are always a function of supply *and* demand. Basic materials prices rose so dramatically because while demand was skyrocketing, supply remained extremely constrained.

### Why Aluminum Lagged

In Table 6.1 you can see that aluminum trailed most other metals during this time period. Its lag wasn't due to lack of demand. Global aluminum consumption increased 36 percent from 2001 through 2006. By comparison, global copper consumption increased only 14 percent over that period.

Prices trailed because supply was rapidly increasing as well. China was forced to become a massive net importer of most industrial metals to satisfy its voracious appetite due to its infrastructure build out. Despite the country's energy constraints, however, it was able to produce aluminum as rapidly as it consumed it. For example, in 2007, its aluminum consumption increased an impressive 34 percent, but its production increased 35 percent. In fact, in just three years from 2004 to 2007, China's aluminum production increased 88 percent! Remember, pricing is always about both supply and demand.

*Source:* Alcan Inc 2006 Annual Report; The World Copper Factbook 2007; World Aluminum Market.

## THE BACKDROP

So why did this happen? Over the 15 years prior to the boom, the mining industry was plagued by underinvestment. Figure 6.1 shows why. Following the inflationary boom of the late 1970s, metal prices dropped dramatically and with them, metal producers' earnings and stock prices. Metal prices and producer earnings rose again in the late 1980s on surging construction, only to quickly fall off again. Recall mines cost billions and require years to develop. Tremendous losses were suffered by those who overzealously expanded output and invested heavily during the previous cycle's height.

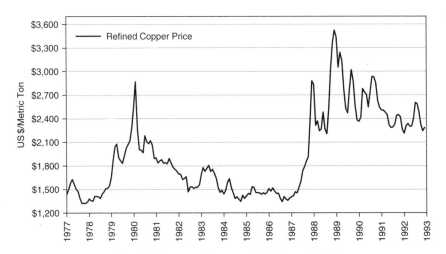

**Figure 6.1   Refined Copper Prices 1977 to 1992**
*Source:* Global Financial Data.

By the 1990s, metal producer executives were determined not to be burned again. This attitude, coupled with a period of low metal prices, caused metal producers to slow expansion. The lack of new projects also meant a lack of opportunity for new workers. The combination of the ongoing Internet revolution and introduction of new financial innovations like derivatives made the mining industry a relative backwater. Many talented and skilled workers shunned the industry, preferring to devote their careers to expanding and better-paying industries with greater opportunities.

Against this backdrop, the fall of the Soviet Union demonstrated capitalism was a more sustainable economic model than communism's controlled economies and led to greater wealth. As capitalism's tenets were adopted and governments largely avoided past mistakes, the emerging markets began stabilizing and growing. For example, Brazil's 85 percent interest rates in 1985 had sunk to 11.25 percent by the start of 2008 as monetary and fiscal policy stabilized, while infrastructure investments surged.[2] Suddenly, global demand for Materials was booming again.

But this time, many metal producers preferred to be "prudent" and shunned new investment, fearing the inevitable bust. Investments in existing mines were delayed and funding for new mines sluggish. This would prove to be a key determinant for higher metal prices since few envisioned the coming strong demand.

## DEMAND GROWTH

The US Census Bureau estimated just over 80 percent of the world's 6.6 billion people lived in emerging market countries in 2007. Consider the need for basic materials if a population this size industrializes, moves to urban settings, and begins consuming the same amount of materials per capita as the developed world. Such a migration doesn't take place in a single year. But the beginning of this migration, and the huge infrastructure investments by governments to facilitate it, created the backbone of the materials consumption increase during the 2003 to 2007 Materials bull market. To understand this period of growth, how it impacted the Materials sector (and the Metals & Mining industry in particular), and what it implies for the future, we need to examine:

- Why governments fund infrastructure investments.
- How infrastructure investments affect basic material consumption.
- Who was industrializing and investing in infrastructure.
- Where the emerging market industrialization process is headed.
- What the developed world contributed to demand and its outlook ahead.

### Running on Two Bucks a Day

While emerging markets have come a long way, it's important to remember just how much further they have to go. Table 6.2 outlines the results of a World Bank study that found 48 percent of the emerging markets population in 2004 was living on less than two dollars a day. Just think of the vast potential wealth creation involved in bringing just a fraction of those folks into the middle class.

### Table 6.2 Emerging Markets Population Living on Less Than $2 a Day

| Region | Population % |
| --- | --- |
| South Asia & India | 77 |
| Sub-Saharan Africa | 72 |
| East Asia, China, & Pacific | 37 |
| Latin America & Caribbean | 22 |
| Middle East & North Africa | 20 |
| Eastern Europe & Central Asia | 10 |
| **Emerging Market Total** | **48** |

Source: World Bank: Absolute Poverty Measure for the Developing World 1981–2004.

## Why Governments Fund Infrastructure Investments

Materials consumption increased dramatically during this period, but why were governments investing so heavily in infrastructure and construction? What was in it for them?

Expenditures on infrastructure are investments, not simply expenses. A significant return can be generated on the investment in the form of higher levels of productivity, increased economic growth rates, higher living standards, reduced income inequality, greater social stability, and of course, higher tax revenues. The World Bank's 2005 Infrastructure Progress Report cited that if Latin America improved its infrastructure to the median level of East Asian countries (or about the level of South Korea), its annual GDP growth rate would increase by 1.4 to 1.8 percent and income inequality would fall by 10 to 20 percent. Such outcomes are obviously appealing.

The World Bank estimates governments provide about 75 percent of infrastructure funding, the private sector provides 20 percent, and international aid and development organizations like the World Bank provide the remaining 5 percent. And although studies vary on the specific degree, they do consistently show that better infrastructure significantly increases productivity. The greatest gains typically come from investments in core infrastructure like transport, power, water, and telecommunications.

## How Infrastructure Investments Impact Basic Materials Consumption

To gain an understanding for the magnitude of infrastructure investments taking place and how they impacted consumption of basic materials, let's take a look at what was actually built.

The following photo shows two satellite photos of the Middle Eastern city of Dubai, one taken in 1973 and the other in 2006. Flush with oil money, the government invested heavily in infrastructure, transforming Dubai City from a barren desert to a city full of skyscrapers with two man-made islands in the shape of palm trees and the world's largest man-made port (the Jebel Ali Harbor). It was estimated in mid-2007 that a quarter of the world's large construction cranes were operating in Dubai.[3] The difference between the two pictures is the difference industrialization has on a society and its consumption of basic materials.

The changes in China were no less dramatic. Examples of its consumption of basic materials include:

**The Industrialization of Dubai**
*Source:* NASA.

- Building the Three Gorges Dam, the largest hydroelectric power plant in the world. It's nearly a mile and half long and took an estimated 27 million cubic meters of concrete and 350,000 tons of steel to build. At full operating capacity, it's designed to produce the power equivalent to 15 nuclear power plants.[4]
- In 2006, China brought on line more new energy capacity each week than the US brought on line all year. At an estimated rate of two gigawatts per plant, China completed over one new power plant a week in 2006 and 2007.[5] This expansion led to a 96 percent increase in China's coal consumption from 2000 through 2007.[6]
- China built its first auto expressway in 1988 and had over 25,000 miles built by the end of 2005. The build-out is estimated to have taken up to 500 million tons of construction aggregate.[7] By comparison, the US had about 47,000 miles of total highways in 2007.[8]

### China's Aggressive Expansion

From 2001 through 2005, the Chinese government spent more on transportation infrastructure than in the previous 50 years combined! And it's not done—China plans to further expand its highway system from 25,000 miles in 2005 to 53,000 miles by 2020. It's also planning 97 new airports between 2007 and 2020, and an increase in port capacity from 2010 to 2020 to allow 85 percent more container traffic.

*Source:* Calum MacLeod, "China's Highways Go the Distance," *USA Today* (January 29, 2006).

### Table 6.3    Passenger and Commercial Vehicle Consumption 2000 to 2005

| Country | Change (%) |
|---------|-----------|
| China | 184 |
| India | 106 |
| Turkey | 104 |
| Brazil | 51 |
| UK | −1 |
| US | −6 |
| **Global Total** | **14** |

*Source:* US Department of Transportation/Research & Innovative Technology Administration, Bureau of Transportation Statistics.

## The Wealth Effect

Infrastructure projects, however, aren't the only consumers of basic materials. Better infrastructure also increases productivity levels, standards of living, and wealth. Increased wealth, higher disposable incomes, and a rising middle class lead to increased consumption of durable goods like autos, appliances, and other consumer goods. As the emerging markets rapidly grew, consumption of these goods soared. This can be seen in Table 6.3, which outlines the growth in passenger and commercial vehicle consumption in select regions from 2000 through 2005.

## Who Was Industrializing and Investing in Infrastructure?

There is no question the acceleration of industrialization in the emerging markets had a dramatic effect on demand for basic materials. From 1980 to 2000, global crude steel production grew 18 percent. In just seven years from 2000 through 2006, global steel production increased 58 percent.[9] But who was actually demanding all of this material?

The answer is more specific than just the emerging markets. It was China. From 2000 through 2006, China's finished steel consumption increased by 187 percent to account for 32 percent of global consumption. The US was a distant second at 11 percent.[10]

China wasn't just consuming steel at an impressive pace, it was also producing it at amazing rates. From 2000 through 2006, China's steel industry grew by an astounding 285 percent to reach 36 percent of global production.[11] Japan was the second largest producer at less than 10 percent.[12] In fact, in order to feed its growing steel habit, China accounted for 95 percent of the growth in iron ore trade from 2000 through 2007 and grew to consume 40 percent of the world's annual iron production.[13]

Due to its massive infrastructure investments, China became the dominant consumer of virtually all major industrial metals. In its 2005 Infrastructure Progress Report, the World Bank estimated the emerging markets as a whole were spending 2 to 4 percent of annual GDP on infrastructure. By comparison, it is estimated China was spending up to 9 percent.

China's footprint can be seen on almost every metal over the period. By the end of 2007, it was the world's largest consumer of copper, iron ore, aluminum, nickel, and zinc. Examples of its metal consumption include:

- Accounting for 60 percent of the growth in copper consumption from 1997 through 2007 to reach 25 percent of global consumption, more than double any other country.[14]
- Accounting for 74 percent of the growth in aluminum consumption from 2000 through 2007 to reach 25 percent of global consumption.
- Accounting for over 90 percent of the growth in nickel consumption from 2000 through 2007.[15]

### Government Intervention

As China began to industrialize, its steel production initially increased significantly faster than consumption, causing its exports to increase rapidly. The growth of China's steel industry was due in part to encouragement from its government through an export subsidy. In June 2007, however, the Chinese government cut the subsidy on many steel exports. It further imposed export taxes at the start of 2008, and China's net steel exports

(*Continued*)

dropped by 27 percent in the first quarter of 2008 when compared to the same period of 2007. (Steel consumption is always compared year over year to account for seasonal variations in construction demand.)

As China's exports declined, raw material costs also increased. Annual iron ore contract prices increased over 65 percent in 2008, while annual coal contract prices increased nearly 200 percent. With a reduction in global supply outside of China and higher production costs that had to be passed on, global steel prices suddenly rose dramatically. As seen in Figure 4.1, however, prices rose faster in the rest of the world than in China. China's extra production was now turned inward, which increased its supply and depressed its regional prices, while the removal of that supply on the global market pushed everyone else's prices higher.

*Source:* Thomson Datastream; "Rio Tinto Secures 85 Percent Rise in 2008 Iron Ore Contract Prices," *Forbes* (June 23, 2008); United Steelworkers, "Australian Rain Plus Chinese Demand Equals Higher Coal Prices," *Steel This Week* (June 5, 2008).

## Where the Emerging Market Industrialization Process Is Headed

Although this case study looks only at the time period from 2003 to 2007, it's worth noting the industrialization boom doesn't stop there. The global population is expected to grow nearly 40 percent from 2007 to 2050 and reach over 9.2 billion people. With 99 percent of the population growth expected to take place in the emerging markets, infrastructure projects must expand just to keep up. As previously mentioned, however, governments have an incentive to do more than just keep up since industrialization brings many benefits.

According to the UN's World Urbanization Prospects report, in 2007 an estimated 49 percent of the world's population lived in an urban environment, but by 2050, an impressive 70 percent of the world's population is expected to live in urban settings.[16] Put another way: While the world's population is expected to increase by almost 40 percent between 2007 and 2050, its urban population will increase by nearly 95 percent. In fact, by 2050 the urban population is expected to reach 6.4 billion and become equivalent to the entire world's population in 2004.[17] This works out to an additional 3.1 billion people moving into urban environments. Construction in housing, roads, bridges, power plants, canals, dams, and other forms of infrastructure will have to expand to an unprecedented scale to meet the challenge. Asia is expected to be the largest contributor to this urban migration with about 60 percent of the increase attributed to it.[18]

## What Urban Population Growth Means for Global Cities

Table 6.4 outlines the United Nation's projections for growth in large urban cities from 2007 to 2025. Over that time, the number of cities in the world with populations over 10 million is expected to grow to 27, a 42 percent increase. For context, consider that in 2007, New York City had a population of just over eight million.

### Table 6.4    Growth in City Density 2007 to 2025

| City Population | Number of Cities, 2007 | Number of Cities, 2025 |
| --- | --- | --- |
| > 10 million | 19 | 27 |
| 5 million to 10 million | 30 | 48 |
| 1 million to 5 million | 382 | 524 |
| 500,000 to 1 million | 460 | 551 |

Source: 2007 UN World Urbanization Prospects.

To meet these growing needs, tremendous sums are expected to be spent on infrastructure around the world. For example:

- In 2008, Xstrata, one of the largest global miners, estimated that $22 trillion would be spent on developing nations' infrastructures over the next decade.[19]
- Emerging markets as a whole will likely need to spend up to 5.5 percent of GDP a year on infrastructure.[20] This translates to about $900 billion a year in infrastructure spending, based just on 2007 GDP levels.
- Rio Tinto, one of the largest mining companies in the world, estimated global consumption of copper would double, while consumption of iron ore and aluminum would increase about 90 percent from 2007 to 2022.[21]

- CSM Worldwide, a leading automotive consulting company, estimated annual global auto production would grow 30 percent from 2007 to 2014, with two-thirds of the growth coming from emerging markets. That translates into an addition of about 550 million passenger cars over the time period.[22] That's more cars than existed globally in 1997.[23]

## What the Developed World Contributed to Demand, and Its Outlook Ahead

In 2005, the American Society of Civil Engineers (ASCE) assessed the condition of the infrastructure in the US and gave it a "D." They estimated it would take $1.6 trillion over the next five years to repair the infrastructure.[24]

Aging infrastructure typically creates little public outcry until it actually fails, but pressure will increase on politicians to rebuild and renew infrastructure in the coming years as deterioration becomes evident. In 2007, a 40-year-old commuter bridge collapsed in Minneapolis, killing 13 people.[25] Earlier that year, an 83-year-old steam pipe in New York City blew a gaping hole in the street during rush hour and injured over 30 people.[26]

### Leaky Pipes

In 2005, the American Society of Civil Engineers estimated six billion gallons of clean drinking water leak out through distribution pipes in the US each day. That's enough water to serve the daily needs of a population the size of California! In 2000, the EPA estimated 72,000 miles of water pipes around the US were over 80 years old and over 400,000 miles more were over 40 years old. The problem is not specific to just the US either. Studies done in Britain in 2006 showed it lost 950 million gallons of clean water a day through its pipes.

*Source:* American Society of Civil Engineers; Erik Sofge and Editors, "The 10 Pieces of U.S. Infrastructure We Must Fix Now," Popular Mechanics (May 2008); Matthew Weaver, "Q&A: Drought," The Guardian (July 4, 2006); US Environmental Protection Agency, Office of Water, "Community Water System Survey 2000," (December 2002).

Crumbling infrastructure doesn't just imperil us, it also retards economic growth, slows productivity, and reduces living standards. It's estimated Americans spend over 3.5 billion hours a year stuck in traffic, largely because one-third of urban roads are congested. It's also estimated this congestion costs motorists over $60 billion a year in wasted time and fuel.[27]

Some efforts have been made to repair the aging infrastructure. In 2005, Congress passed the $286 billion Federal Highway Bill to help address the growing needs of our highway system; while in 2006, California voters approved a $42.7 billion bond package to begin addressing the state's infrastructure needs.[28] Table 6.5 outlines the combined growth of public and private spending in the US on the primary infrastructure categories from 2003 through 2007. Total US infrastructure spending increased a significant 37 percent in these categories over the five-year period.

As public awareness of the developed world's infrastructure needs increases, government funded construction projects are only likely to increase. When combined with the industrialization of emerging markets, the demand for basic materials has placed a strain on the world's resources we've rarely, if ever, seen before.

### Table 6.5    US Infrastructure Spending 2003–2007

| Category | Change (%) |
|---|---|
| Communication | 102 |
| Public Safety | 61 |
| Sewage & Waste Disposal | 55 |
| Transportation | 35 |
| Highway & Street | 28 |
| Power | 28 |
| Water Supply | 10 |
| **Weighted Total** | **37** |

*Source:* Thomson Datastream; US Census Bureau.

## SUPPLY CONSTRAINTS

As demand surged to unprecedented levels from 2003 to 2007, supply struggled to keep up. Haunted by past cycles, producers refused to aggressively expand production. Even after finally recognizing the scope of demand growth and growing investment in new developments, expansion was held back by a host of factors, including:

- Lack of skilled labor
- Lack of equipment
- Infrastructure bottlenecks and declining ore grades
- The shift to less developed regions
  - Regulation and nationalization
  - Power constraints
  - Labor strife
- Environmental regulations

### Lack of Skilled Labor

By the time firms decided to expand, they found the previous 15 years of underinvestment throughout the industry had resulted in a severe lack of experienced and skilled workers. Greg Wilkins, CEO of Barrick Gold, the largest gold producer in the world, said in the company's Q4 2006 conference call, "asked what's one of the biggest things that keep you awake at night, my answer is really people, because the industry is short of good quality people."[29]

Growth opportunities will no doubt attract new talent, but developing skills and experience takes time. The skilled labor shortage raised costs and delayed projects in the last decade, which significantly slowed attempts to increase production and catch up with soaring demand.

### Lack of Equipment

Access to equipment was also an issue since mining firms weren't the only ones burned in the past. Mining equipment producers also suffered through previous cycles. So as mining firms finally attempted to expand production, equipment makers didn't follow suit. Significant

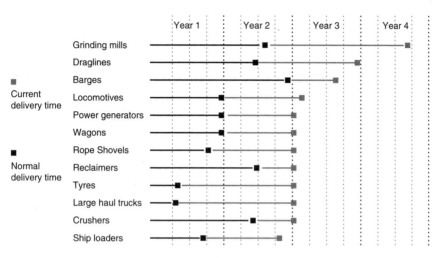

**Figure 6.2    Acute Equipment Shortages Constrain Metal Supply**
*Source:* 2007 Rio Tinto estimates; reprinted with permission from Rio Tinto.

order backlogs and delays followed. Equipment simply couldn't be produced fast enough to keep up with demand. Figure 6.2 outlines the delays Rio Tinto faced in 2007 to procure equipment. The delivery time for locomotives and power generators doubled from one year to two. Ordering large haul trucks and tires was even worse, with delivery times stretching from six months to 2.5 years.

Equipment was so scarce, firms took what they could get. Deliveries of 60-ton mining trucks *without tires* were commonplace. Costs also skyrocketed. For example, prices of 12-foot mining tires practically quadrupled, reaching up to $40,000 per tire by 2006. As with the dearth of skilled labor, equipment shortages raised costs and delayed projects.[30]

### Miners Need Tires

Barrick Gold, the largest gold miner in the world, estimated it spent about $80 million on tires in 2006. Its largest tires cost up to $60,000 apiece, and it expects its purchases of "giant" tires (45 inches tall and larger) to increase by 50 percent between 2007 and 2012, reaching 4,500 purchases a year.

*(Continued)*

To help alleviate its tire shortage, Barrick Gold took an extraordinary step in early 2008. It financed the expansion of a tire producer (Yokohama Rubber) with a $35 million loan and signed a 10-year contract to purchase 1,300 giant tires a year to help ensure the tire producer would generate an adequate long-term return on the expansion. For a refresher on just how big the largest of these tires are, recall the picture of the giant mining truck in Chapter 1. Only a few producers in the world are capable of manufacturing tires of that size.

*Source:* "Barrick Signs Innovative 10-year Agreement with Yokohama to Secure Tire Supply," Barrick Gold Corporation Press Release, (January 30, 2008).

## Infrastructure Bottlenecks and Declining Ore Grades

Another roadblock was the lack of sufficient infrastructure to transport raw materials once they had been mined. Existing ports and railroads were unprepared to handle the new surge in demand—it doesn't do much good to expand production if you can't transport it to customers. In early 2007, a queue of 67 ships was reported off Australia's largest coal port. The backlog took months to clear. Major infrastructure expansions were initiated to help alleviate such bottlenecks, but construction projects of the required scale take years to complete and have been slow to catch up with demand.[31]

Tied to the lack of infrastructure capacity was simply a lack of new mines. The underinvestment in the mining sector during the 1990s also resulted in very limited exploration and new development. Many existing mines had aged, and ore grades (the percentage of metal per ton of rock mined) were declining. After all, the most profitable and highest grade regions are typically mined first. This caused costs to rise (it's more expensive to mine two tons of rock for one pound of metal than one ton of rock for two pounds of metal) and constrained production.

## The Shift to Less Developed Regions

When the miners did go looking for new mines, they were also forced into less stable regions. Most high-quality mineral deposits in the developed world were already exploited. To find new high-quality deposits, miners were forced into emerging markets and their higher risk business environments.

Many developing regions continued to struggle with corruption, political instability, weak property rights, and labor strife. Limited existing infrastructure in many emerging market countries also posed a challenge. The cost and time to develop a new mine are significantly higher if a firm has to build its own roads, ports, power plants, and rail systems rather than simply renting space on pre-existing infrastructure. The higher risks and costs further delayed development of new mines and constrained production.

**Regulation**    One of the largest risks of doing business in less stable emerging markets is regulations, which can change at politicians' whims or with a newly elected government. A host of regulations can be modified, including mining licenses, taxes, royalties, ownership stakes, and tariffs, but three types have been particularly relevant in recent years.

- **Nationalization:** From an owner's perspective, the worst move a government can make is to nationalize an operation. The owner (including shareholders) typically receives little or no compensation because the government confiscates their mines, equipment, and manufacturing plants. Examples include Uzbekistan taking Newmont Mining's gold mine and assets in 2007, and Venezuela taking over the country's steel and cement industry in early 2008.[32]
- **Windfall taxes:** As outlined in Chapter 1, governments typically tax mining companies for a percentage of their sales or output. Windfall taxes are extra taxes mining firms are forced to pay during periods of strong earnings. After Peru elected a new president in 2006, mining companies agreed to pay $757 million in equal installments over the next five years in a "voluntary payment" to retain mining rights. The payments were in addition to normal royalty fees. The miners also pledged to invest at least $10 billion in new mines in Peru over the same time

span.[33] A similar event happened in Mongolia in 2006 when the government suddenly imposed a 68 percent windfall tax on mining proceeds of gold and copper when prices exceeded set levels.[34]

- **Import and export taxes:** At various times, export and import taxes also changed suddenly, altering the landscape of an investment environment. For example, in 2007 India implemented export taxes on iron ore. The growth rate of iron ore exports to China, where 80 percent of India's iron ore exports go, subsequently fell from about 20 percent to 5 percent.[35]

High levels of political risk can be a tremendous challenge when trying to justify spending billions of dollars and forecasting an expected rate of return on an investment. In many cases during the 2003–2007 Materials bull market, it delayed or deterred investments altogether and significantly constrained production growth.

### Governments: Friend or Foe?

While government intervention is rarely beneficial for the industry, it can occasionally be beneficial for specific companies. This was the case in Russia with the auction of major coal deposits in 2007. Arcelor-Mittal, the largest steel producer in the world, was prepared to bid for the assets to help vertically integrate its steelmaking operations. Only days before the auction, however, it was barred from participating by the Russian government in an effort to keep the assets in Russian hands. The removal of such a formidable bidder helped Mechel, a much smaller Russian steel producer, win the auction.

*Source:* Agence France-Presse, "ArcelorMittal Excluded From Russian Mine Auction," *Industry Week* (October 8, 2007).

**Power Constraints** Power constraints posed another challenge. Recall from Chapter 1 that mining is generally energy intensive. While power plants were rapidly constructed globally, not all areas participated equally and many increased consumption as fast as they increased production. When a power grid is running at full capacity, any slight disruption can create rolling blackouts or power rationing.

In early 2008, South Africa's utility provider Eskom had a power failure and was forced to temporarily shut down. This was mostly the result of years of underinvestment by the government. It quickly resumed power, but said for the next four years, it would only be able to provide between 90 and 95 percent of what was previously provided.

The significance of such problems to global metal production was visible in platinum prices (80 percent of the world's platinum is produced in South Africa). Following the power cuts, platinum prices rose nearly 45 percent in the following month and a half.[36]

**Labor Strife**    Labor concerns, specifically regarding unionized labor, were a constant source of frustration for mining firms. As metal prices and miners' profits increased, labor unions were increasingly vocal about wanting a share of the profits. Strikes over pay and safety conditions were practically monthly events.

Many companies agreed to pay higher wages and one-time bonuses to prevent or settle strikes. This increased the cost of production and in some cases deterred firms from expanding mines in areas with high labor unrest. Strikes also frustrated analysts since the length and severity of such disruptions were difficult to predict.

## Environmental Regulations

The last challenge we'll cover relates to the environment. Recall from Chapter 1 that separating the metal from the rock and other impurities is often a messy business involving chemicals such as sulfuric acid, arsenic, and cyanide. When the waste product is discarded, it can poison water sources and the surrounding flora and fauna. Companies must provide detailed plans as to how they will dispose of the waste products prior to receiving governmental permits. Should they deviate from the plans or pollute the surrounding environment, they are generally liable for damages.

One of the more prominent cases during the period involved a gold mine in Indonesia owned by Newmont Mining. The tailings (or leftover rock, after it had been processed with toxic chemicals) were deposited in the middle of a nearby bay through an underwater pipe extending half a mile into the water. In 2004, local residents began complaining the toxins were polluting the bay and causing illnesses and skin rashes.

The bay was found to have an unusually high level of mercury and arsenic. Civil and criminal proceedings were brought against the firm and its directors, with some being detained in Indonesia for extended periods of time and threatened with up to three years in prison. Ultimately, the company and directors were found innocent of criminal charges, the civil suit was dropped, and the company agreed to pay $30 million to the Indonesian government to help clean up the area and provide aid to the affected community.[37]

All of these risks and challenges served to severely stunt production growth in the midst of soaring demand. The result was dramatically higher raw material prices.

## THE GROWTH OF MERGERS AND ACQUISITIONS

The uncertainty, risks, and costs surrounding the expansion of production during this period were significant. The greater the risk and uncertainty on generating a return on an investment, the more hesitant investors will be to provide funding. The simultaneous unavailability of skilled labor and equipment simply compounded the problem and further delayed new production.

This environment of constrained supply growth and rising demand caused firms to purchase existing mines rather than taking on the risk of developing new mines. A favorable credit environment also provided a friendly environment for M&A transactions and deals flourished. Table 6.6 outlines the year-over-year increase in announced deal value and volume for the global Metals & Mining industry. The announced deal value in 2007 of $339 billion was an amazing 3,359 percent higher than in 2002, prior to the start of the Materials bull market. It also wasn't just a few big deals. In 2007, an

## Table 6.6    Year-Over-Year Growth in Global Metals & Mining M&A

| Year | Change in Deal Value (%) | Change in Number of Deals (%) |
|---|---|---|
| 2003 | 144 | 150 |
| 2004 | −37 | −38 |
| 2005 | 226 | 224 |
| 2006 | 238 | 238 |
| 2007 | 105 | 105 |
| Change from 2002 to 2007 | 3,359 | 3,419 |

*Source:* Thomson Reuters; as of 12/31/07, deal value and volume include public and private transactions.

impressive 1,010 deals were announced, representing a 3,419 percent increase over 2002.[38]

### Chapter Recap

The 2003 to 2007 bull market in Materials (and Metals & Mining in particular) was characterized by tremendous demand growth for basic materials and significant supply constraints due to years of previous underinvestment. It was led by tremendous infrastructure build-outs tied to accelerating growth and industrialization in emerging markets and supported by the rebuilding of infrastructure in the developed world. In particular, China's tremendous investment in infrastructure served as the primary force behind rising global metal consumption.

Industrialization of emerging markets, however, is not complete, and tremendous growth opportunities still exist for both the Materials sector and emerging markets themselves. The degree to which governments embrace industrialization and invest in infrastructure in both emerging markets and the developed world will be a major determinant of basic material consumption growth over the next 20 or 30 years. The ability to navigate the many risks, uncertainties, and high costs surrounding production growth will also continue to play a major role in the success of producers to capitalize on any growth that does take place.

- Supply constraints existed from years of previous underinvestment and fears of short boom and bust cycles.

(Continued)

- Labor and equipment were in short supply due to lack of capacity from previous underinvestment.
- Demand suddenly surged due to the industrialization of the emerging markets, led by China.
- Demand growth was supported by infrastructure rebuilds in the developed world.
- Search for new production pushed miners into less stable regions with high risks and uncertainties.
- Costs rose and production suffered, leading to a surge in acquisitions of existing producers with less uncertainty.

# III

# THINKING LIKE A PORTFOLIO MANAGER

# 7

# THE TOP-DOWN METHOD

**S**o if you're bullish on Materials, how much of your portfolio should you put in Materials stocks? Twenty-five percent? Fifty? One hundred percent? This question concerns portfolio management. Most investors concern themselves only with individual companies ("I like US Steel, so I'll buy some"), without considering how it fits into their overall portfolio. But this is no way to manage your money.

In this part of the book, we show you how to analyze Materials companies like a top-down portfolio manager. This includes a full description of the top-down method, how to use benchmarks, and how the top-down method applies to the Materials sector. We then delve into security analysis in Chapter 8, where we provide a framework for analyzing any company, and discuss many of the important questions to ask when analyzing Materials companies. Finally, in Chapter 9, we conclude by giving a few examples of specific investing strategies for the Materials sector.

## INVESTING IS A SCIENCE

Too many investors today think investing has "rules"—that all one must do to succeed in investing for the long run is find the right set of investing rules. But that simply doesn't work. Why? All well-known and widely discussed information is already reflected in stock prices. This is a basic tenet of market theory and commonly referred to as "market efficiency." So if you see a headline about a stock you follow, there's no use trading on that information—it's already priced in. You missed the move.

If everything known is already discounted in prices, the only way to consistently beat the market is to know something others don't. Think about it: There are many intelligent investors and longtime professionals who fail to beat the market year after year, most with the same access to information as anyone, if not more. Why?

Most view investing as a craft. They think, "If I learn the craft of value investing and all its rules, then I can be a successful investor using that method." But that simply can't work because by definition, all the conventional ways of thinking about value investing will already be widely known and thus priced in. In fact, most investment styles are very well-known and already widely practiced. There are undoubtedly millions of investors out there much like you, looking at the same metrics and information you are. So there isn't much power in them. Even the investing techniques themselves are widely known—taught to millions in universities and practiced by hundreds of thousands of professionals globally. There's no edge.

Moreover, it's been demonstrated investment styles move in and out of favor over time—no one style or category is inherently better than another in the long run. You may think "value" investing works wonders to beat markets, but the fact is growth stocks will trounce value at times.

The key to beating stock markets lies in being dynamic—never adhering for all time to a single investment idea—and gleaning information the market hasn't yet priced in. In other words, you cannot adhere to a single set of "rules" and hope to outperform markets over time.

So how can you beat the markets? By thinking of investing as a science.

## Einstein's Brain and the Stock Market

If he weren't so busy becoming the most renowned scientist of the twentieth century, Albert Einstein would have made a killing on Wall Street—but not because he had such a high IQ. Granted, he was immensely intelligent, but a high IQ alone does not make a market guru. (If it did, MIT professors would be making millions managing money instead of teaching.) Instead, it's the style of his thought and the method of his work that matter.

In the little we know about Einstein's investment track record, he didn't do very well. He lost most of his Nobel Prize money in bad bond ventures.[1] Heck, Sir Isaac Newton may have given us the three laws of motion, but even his talents didn't extend to investing. He lost his shirt in the South Sea Bubble of the early 1700s, explaining later, "I can calculate the movement of the stars, but not the madness of men."[2]

So why believe Einstein would have been a great portfolio manager if he put his mind to it? In short, Einstein was a true and highly creative scientist. He didn't take the acknowledged rules of physics as such—he used prior knowledge, logic, and creativity combined with the rigors of verifiable, testable scientific method to create an entirely new view of the cosmos. In other words, he was dynamic and gleaned knowledge others didn't have. Investors should do the same. (Not to worry, you won't need advanced calculus to do it.)

Einstein's unique character gave him an edge—he truly had a mind made to beat markets. Scientists have studied his work, his speeches, his letters, even his brain (literally) to find the secret of his intellect. In all, his approach to information processing and idea generation, his willingness to go against the grain of the establishment, and his relentless pursuit of answers to questions no one else was asking ultimately made him a genius.

Both his contemporaries and most biographers agree one of Einstein's foremost gifts was his ability to discern "the big picture." Unlike many scientists who could easily drown themselves in data minutiae, Einstein had an ability to see above the fray. Another way to say this is he could take the same information everyone else at his time was looking at and interpret it differently, yet correctly. He accomplished this using his talent for extracting the most important data from what he studied and linking them together in innovative ways no one else could.

Einstein called this "combinatory play." Similar to a child experimenting with a new Lego set, Einstein would combine and recombine seemingly unrelated ideas, concepts, and images to produce new, original discoveries. In the end, most all new ideas are merely the combination of existing ones in one form or another. Take $E = mc^2$: Einstein was not the first to discover the concepts of energy, mass, or the speed of light; rather, he combined these concepts in a novel way, and in the process, altered the way in which we view the universe.[3]

Einstein's combinatory play is a terrific metaphor for stock investing. To be a successful market strategist, you must be able to extract the most important data from all of the "noise" permeating today's markets and generate conclusions the market hasn't yet appreciated. Central to this task is your ability to link data together in unique ways and produce new insights and themes for your portfolio in the process.

Einstein learned science basics just like his peers. But once he had those mastered, he directed his brain to challenging prior assumptions and inventing entirely different lenses to look through.

This is why this book isn't intended to give you a "silver bullet" for picking the right Materials stocks. The fact is the "right" Materials stocks will be different in different times and situations. You don't have to be Einstein, you just should think differently—and like a scientist—if you want to beat markets.

## THE TOP-DOWN METHOD

Overwhelmingly, investment professionals today do what can broadly be labeled "bottom-up" investing. Their emphasis is on stock selection. A typical bottom-up investor researches an assortment of companies and attempts to pick those with the greatest likelihood of outperforming the market based on individual merits. The selected securities are cobbled together to form a portfolio, and factors like country and economic sector exposure are purely residuals of security selection, not planned decisions.

"Top-down" investing reverses the order. A top-down investor first analyzes big picture factors like economics, politics, and sentiment to forecast which investment categories are most likely to outperform the market. Only then does a top-down investor begin looking at individual securities. Top-down investing is inevitably more concerned with a portfolio's aggregate exposure to investment categories than with any individual security. Thus, top-down is an inherently *dynamic* mode of investment because investment strategies are based upon the prevailing market and economic environment (which changes often).

There's significant debate in the investment community as to which approach is superior. This book's goal is not to reject bottom-up investing—there are indeed investors who've successfully utilized bottom-up approaches. Rather, the goal is to introduce a comprehensive and flexible methodology that any investor could use to build a portfolio designed to beat the global stock market in any investment environment. It's a framework for gleaning new insights and making good on information not already reflected in stock prices.

Before we describe the method, let's explore several key reasons why a top-down approach is advantageous:

- **Scalability:** A bottom-up process is akin to looking for needles in a haystack. A top-down process is akin to seeking the haystacks with the highest concentration of needles. Globally, there are nearly 25,000 publicly traded stocks. Even the largest institutions with the greatest research resources cannot hope to adequately examine all these companies. Smaller institutions and individual investors must prioritize where to focus their limited resources. Unlike a bottom-up process, a top-down process makes this gargantuan task manageable by determining, upfront, what slices of the market to examine at the security level.
- **Enhanced stock selection:** Well-designed top-down processes generate insights that can greatly enhance stock selection.

Macroeconomic or political analysis, for instance, can help determine what types of strategic attributes will face head- or tailwinds (see Chapter 8 for a full explanation).

- **Risk control:** Bottom-up processes are highly subject to unintended risk concentrations. Top-down processes are inherently better suited to manage risk exposures throughout the investment process.

- **Macro overview:** Top-down processes are more conducive to avoiding macro-driven calamities like the bursting of the Japan bubble in the 1990s, the Technology bubble in 2000, or the bear market of 2000 to 2002. No matter how good an individual company may be, it is still beholden to sector, regional, and broad market factors. In fact, there is evidence "macro" factors can largely determine a stock's performance regardless of individual merit.

## Top-Down Means Thinking 70-20-10

A top-down investment process also helps focus on what's most important to investment results: asset allocation and sub-asset allocation decisions. Many investors focus most of their attention on security-level portfolio decisions, like picking individual stocks they think will perform well. However, studies have shown that over 90 percent of return variability is derived from asset allocation decisions, not market timing or stock selection.[4]

*Our research shows about 70 percent of return variability is derived from asset allocation, 20 percent from sub-asset allocation (such as country, sector, size, and style), and 10 percent from security selection.* While security selection can make a significant difference over time, higher-level portfolio decisions dominate investment results more often than not.

The balance of this chapter defines the various steps in the top-down method, specifically as they relate to making country, sector, and style decisions. This same basic framework can be applied to portfolios to make allocations within sectors. At the end of the chapter, we detail how this framework can be applied to the Materials sector.

## Benchmarks

A key part of the top-down model is using benchmarks. A benchmark is typically a broad-based index of securities such as the S&P 500, MSCI World, or Russell 2000. Benchmarks are indispensible road maps for structuring a portfolio, monitoring risk, and judging performance over time.

Tactically, a portfolio should be structured to maximize the probability of consistently beating the benchmark. This is inherently different than maximizing returns. Unlike aiming to achieve some fixed rate of return each year, which will cause disappointment relative to peers when capital markets are very strong and is potentially unrealistic when the capital markets are very weak, a properly benchmarked portfolio provides a realistic guide for dealing with uncertain market conditions.

Portfolio construction begins by evaluating the characteristics of the chosen benchmark: sector weights, country weights, and market cap and valuations. Then an expected risk and return is assigned to each of these segments (based on portfolio drivers), and the most attractive areas are overweighted, while the least attractive are underweighted. Table 7.1 shows MSCI World benchmark sector characteristics as of December 31, 2007 as an example, while Table 7.2

### Table 7.1    MSCI World Characteristics: Sectors

| Sector | Weight (%) |
|---|---|
| Financials | 22.6 |
| Industrials | 11.4 |
| Information Technology | 11.0 |
| Energy | 10.9 |
| Consumer Discretionary | 9.8 |
| Consumer Staples | 8.8 |
| Health Care | 8.7 |
| Materials | 7.2 |
| Telecommunication | 4.9 |
| Utilities | 4.7 |

*Source:* Thomson Datastream; MSCI, Inc.[5] as of 12/31/07.

### Table 7.2  MSCI World Characteristics: Countries

| Country | Weight (%) |
| --- | --- |
| US | 47.1 |
| UK | 10.8 |
| Japan | 9.7 |
| France | 5.2 |
| Germany | 4.6 |
| Canada | 4.1 |
| Switzerland | 3.3 |
| Australia | 3.2 |
| Spain | 2.1 |
| Italy | 1.9 |
| Netherlands | 1.4 |
| Hong Kong | 1.2 |
| Sweden | 1.1 |
| Finland | 0.9 |
| Belgium | 0.6 |
| Singapore | 0.5 |
| Norway | 0.5 |
| Denmark | 0.5 |
| Greece | 0.4 |
| Ireland | 0.3 |
| Austria | 0.3 |
| Portugal | 0.2 |
| New Zealand | 0.1 |
| Emerging Markets | 0.0 |

*Source:* Thomson Datastream; MSCI, Inc.[6] as of 12/31/07.

shows country characteristics, and Table 7.3 shows market cap and valuations.

Based on benchmark characteristics, portfolio drivers are then used to determine country, sector, and style decisions for the portfolio. For example, in Table 7.1 the Financials sector weight of the MSCI World Index is about 23 percent. Therefore, a portfolio

**Table 7.3    MSCI World Characteristics: Market Cap and Valuations**

|                              | Valuations     |
| ---------------------------- | -------------- |
| Median Market Cap            | $7.3 Billion   |
| Weighted Average Market Cap  | $80.9 Billion  |
| P/E                          | 15.5           |
| P/B                          | 2.6            |
| Div Yield                    | 2.3            |
| P/CF                         | 12.7           |
| P/S                          | 2.4            |
| Number of Holdings           | 1,959          |

*Source:* Thomson Datastream; MSCI, Inc.[7] as of 12/31/07.

*Note:* P/E = price-to-earnings ratio; P/B = price-to-book ratio; Div Yield = dividend yield; P/CF = price-to-cash-flow ratio; P/S = price-to-sales ratio.

managed against this benchmark would consider a 23 percent weight in Financials "neutral," or market-weighted. If you believe Financials will perform better than the market in the foreseeable future, then you would "overweight" the sector, or hold more than 23 percent of your portfolio in Financials stocks. The reverse is true for an "under-weight"—you'd hold less than 23 percent in Financials if you were pessimistic on the sector looking ahead.

Note that being pessimistic on Financials *doesn't necessarily mean holding zero financial stocks.* It might only mean holding a lesser per-centage of stocks in your portfolio than the benchmark. This is an important feature of benchmarking—it allows an investor to make strategic decisions on sectors and countries, but maintains diversifica-tion, thus managing risk more appropriately.

For the Materials sector, we can use Materials-specific benchmarks like the S&P 500 Materials, MSCI World Materials, or Russell 2000 Materials indexes. The components of these benchmarks can then be evaluated at a more detailed level such as industry and sub-industry weights. (For example, we broke out MSCI World industry and sub-industry benchmark weights in Chapter 4.)

## TOP-DOWN DECONSTRUCTED

The top-down method begins by first analyzing the macro environment. It asks the "big" questions like: Do you think stocks will go up or down in the next 12 months? If so, which countries or sectors should benefit most? Once you have decided on these high-level portfolio "drivers" (sometimes called "themes"), you can examine various macro portfolio drivers to make general overweight and underweight decisions for countries, sectors, industries, and sub-industries versus your benchmark.

For instance, let's say we've determined a macroeconomic driver that goes something like this: "In the next 12 months, I believe global infrastructure construction will be greater than most expect." That's a very high-level statement with important implications for your portfolio. It means you'd want to search for industries, and ultimately stocks, that would benefit most from increased infrastructure construction.

The second step in top-down is applying quantitative screening criteria to narrow the choice set of stocks. Since, in our hypothetical example, we believe infrastructure construction will be high, it likely means we're bullish on Metals & Mining stocks. But which ones? Are you bullish on, say, copper producers? Aluminum producers? Steel producers? Do you want producers with exposure to the US or another region? Do you want small cap Materials companies or large cap? And what about valuations? Are you looking for growth or value? (Size and growth/value categories are often referred to as "style" decisions.) These criteria and more can help you narrow the list of stocks you might buy.

The third and final step is performing fundamental analysis on individual stocks. Notice that a great deal of thinking, analysis, and work is done before you ever think about individual stocks. That's the key to the top-down approach: It emphasizes high-level themes and funnels its way down to individual stocks, as is illustrated in Figure 7.1.

### Step 1: Analyze Portfolio Drivers and Country and Sector Selection

Let's examine the first step in the top-down method more closely. In order to make top-down decisions, we develop and analyze what

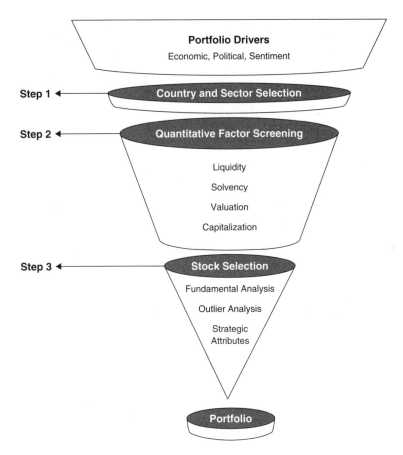

**Figure 7.1    Portfolio Drivers**

we call *portfolio drivers* (as mentioned previously). We segment these portfolio drivers in three general categories: *economic, political,* and *sentiment.*

Portfolio drivers are what drive the performance of a broad category of stocks. Accurately identifying current and future drivers will help you find areas of the market most likely to outperform or underperform your benchmark (i.e., the broader stock market).

Table 7.4 shows examples of each type of portfolio driver. It's important to note these drivers are by no means comprehensive nor are they valid for all time periods. In fact, correctly identifying new portfolio drivers is essential to beating the market in the long term.

## Table 7.4   Portfolio Drivers

| Economic | Political | Sentiment |
|---|---|---|
| Yield curve spread | Taxation | Mutual fund flows |
| Relative GDP growth | Property rights | Relative style and asset class valuations |
| Monetary base/growth | Structural reform | Media coverage |
| Currency strength | Privatization | Institutional searches |
| Relative interest rates | Trade/capital barriers | Consumer confidence |
| Inflation | Current account | Foreign investment |
| Debt level (sovereign, corporate, consumer) | Government stability | Professional investor forecasts |
| Infrastructure spending | Political turnover | Momentum cycle analysis |
| M&A, issuance and repurchase activity | Wars/conflicts | Risk aversion |

**Economic Drivers**   Economic drivers are anything related to the macroeconomic environment. This could include monetary policy, interest rates, lending activity, yield curve analysis, relative GDP growth analysis, and myriad others. What economic forces are likely to drive GDP growth throughout countries in the world? What is the outlook for interest rates and how would that impact sectors? What is the outlook for technology and infrastructure spending among countries?

Economic drivers pertain not only to the fundamental outlook of the economy (GDP growth, interest rates, inflation), but also to the stock market (valuations, M&A activity, share buybacks). As an investor, it's your job to identify these drivers, and determine how they'll impact your overall portfolio and each of its segments.

The following is an example list of economic drivers that could impact portfolio performance:

- US economic growth will be higher than consensus expectations.
- European Union interest rates will remain benign.
- Mergers, acquisitions, and share buybacks will remain strong.
- Emerging markets growth will drive commodity demand.

**Political Drivers**   Political drivers can be country-specific, pertain to regions (European Union, Organisation for Economic Cooperation and Development [OECD]), or affect interaction between countries or regions (such as trade policies). These drivers are more concerned with categories such as taxation, government stability, fiscal policy, and political turnover. Which countries are experiencing a change in government that could have a meaningful impact on their economies? Which sectors could be at risk from new taxation or legislation? Which countries are undergoing pro-growth reforms?

Political drivers will help determine the relative attractiveness of market segments and countries based on the outlook for the political environment. Be warned, however: Most investors suffer from "home country bias," where they ascribe too much emphasis on the politics of their own country. Always keep in mind it's a big, interconnected world out there, and geopolitical developments everywhere can have implications.

What are possible political drivers you can find? The following is a list of examples that can drive stocks up or down:

- Political party change in Japan driving pro-growth reforms.
- New tax policies in Germany stalling economic growth.
- Protests, government coups, conflict driving political instability in Thailand.

**Sentiment Drivers**   Sentiment drivers attempt to measure consensus thinking about investment categories. Ideally, drivers identify market opportunities where sentiment is different than reality. For example, let's say you observe current broad market sentiment expects a US recession in the next year. But you disagree and believe GDP growth will be strong. This presents an excellent opportunity for excess returns. You can load up on stocks that will benefit from an economic boom and watch the prices rise as the rest of the market realizes it much later.

Since the market is a discounter of all known information, it's important to try and identify what the market is pricing in. The interpretation of such investor drivers is typically counterintuitive (avoid what is overly popular and seek what is largely unpopular). Looking forward, which sectors are investors most bullish about and why? What countries or sectors are widely discussed in the media? What market segments have been bid up recently based on something other than fundamentals? If the market's perception is different than fundamentals in the short term, stocks will eventually correct themselves to reflect reality in the long term.

A note of caution: Gauging market sentiment does not mean being a *contrarian*. Contrarians are investors who simply do the opposite of what most believe will happen. Instead, find places where sentiment (people's beliefs) doesn't match what you believe is reality and over- or underweight sections of your portfolio accordingly, relative to your benchmark. Examples of sentiment drivers include:

- Investors remain pessimistic about Technology despite improving fundamentals.
- Sentiment for the Chinese stock market approaching euphoria, stretching valuations.
- Professional investors universally forecast US small cap stocks to outperform.

### How to Create Your Own Investment Drivers

In order to form your own investment drivers, the first step is accessing a wide array of data from multiple sources. For country drivers, this could range from globally focused publications like the *Wall Street Journal* or *Financial Times* to regional newspapers or government data. For sector drivers, this could include reading trade publications or following major company announcements.

Remember, however, that markets are efficient—they reflect all widely known information. Most pertinent information about public companies is, well, *public*. Which means the market already knows. News travels fast, and investors with the knowledge and expectations are absorbed by markets very quickly. Those seeking to profit on a bit of news, rumor, or speculation must acknowledge the market will probably move faster than they can. Therefore, in order to consistently generate excess returns, you must either know something others don't or interpret widely known information differently and correctly from the crowd. (For a detailed discussion on these factors and more, read *The Only Three Questions That Count* by Ken Fisher.)

## Step 2: Quantitative Factor Screening

Step two in the top-down method is screening for quantitative factors. This allows you to narrow the potential list of stocks once your portfolio drivers are in place.

There are thousands and thousands of stocks out there, so it's vital to use a series of factors like market capitalization and valuations to narrow the field a bit. Securities passing this screen are then subjected to further quantitative analysis that eliminates companies with excessive risk profiles relative to their peer group, such as companies with excessive leverage or balance sheet risk and securities lacking sufficient liquidity for investment.

The rigidity of the quantitative screens is entirely up to you, and will determine the number of companies on your prospect list. The more rigid the criteria, the fewer the companies that make the list. Broader criteria will increase the number of companies.

**Examples**   How can you perform such a screen? Here are two examples of quantitative factor screenings to show how broad or specific you can be. You might want to apply very strict criteria, or you may prefer to be broader.

### Strict Criteria

- First, you decide you want to search for only Materials firms. By definition, that excludes all companies from the other nine sectors. Already, you've narrowed the field a lot!
- Now, let's say that based on your high-level drivers, you only want European Materials stocks. By excluding all other regions besides Europe, you've narrowed the field even more.
- Next, let's decide to search only for Steel firms in the Materials sector.
- Perhaps you don't believe very small stocks are preferable, so you limit market capitalization to $5 billion and above.
- Lastly, let's set some parameters for valuation:
  - P/E (price-to-earnings) less than 12
  - P/B (price-to-book) less than 8

- P/CF (price-to-cash-flow) less than 10
- P/S (price-to-sales) less than 10

This rigorous process of selecting parameters will yield a small number of stocks to research, all based on your higher-level themes. But maybe you have a reason to be less specific and want to do a broader screen because you think Materials in general is a good place to be.

### Broad Criteria

- Materials sector
- Global (no country or region restrictions)
- Market caps above $10 billion

This selection process is much broader and obviously gives you a much longer list of stocks to choose from. Doing either a strict or broad screen isn't inherently better. It just depends on how well-formed and specific your higher-level themes are. Obviously, a stricter screen means less work for you in step three—actual stock selection.

## Step 3: Stock Selection

After narrowing the prospect list, your final step is identifying individual securities possessing strategic attributes consistent with higher-level portfolio themes. (We'll cover the stock selection process specifically in more detail in Chapter 8.) Your stock selection process should attempt to accomplish two goals:

1. Find firms possessing strategic attributes consistent with higher-level portfolio themes, derived from the drivers that give those firms a competitive advantage versus their peers. For example, if you believe owning firms with dominant market shares in consolidating industries is a favorable characteristic, you would search for firms with that profile.
2. Maximize the likelihood of beating the category of stocks you are analyzing. For example, if you want a certain portfolio

weight of Diversified Mining companies and need 4 stocks out of 12 meeting the quantitative criteria, you then pick the 4 that, as a group, maximize the likelihood of beating all 12 as a whole. This is different than trying to pick "the best four." By avoiding stocks likely to be extreme or "weird" outliers versus the group, you can reduce portfolio risk while adding value at the security selection level.

In lieu of picking individual securities, there are other ways to exploit high-level themes in the top-down process. For instance, if you feel strongly about a particular sub-industry but don't think you can add value through individual security analysis, it may be more prudent to buy a group of companies in the sub-industry or a category product like an exchange-traded fund (ETF). There are a growing variety of ETFs that track the domestic and global Materials sector, industries, and even specific commodity prices. This way, you can be sure to gain broad Materials exposure without much stock-specific risk. (For more information on ETFs, visit www.ishares.com, www. sectorspdr.com, or www.masterdata.com.)

## MANAGING AGAINST A MATERIALS BENCHMARK

Now we can practice translating this specifically to your Materials allocation. Just as you analyze the components of your benchmark to determine country and sector components in a top-down strategy, you must analyze each sector's components, as we did in Chapter 4. To demonstrate how, we'll use the MSCI World Materials Sector index as the benchmark. Table 7.5 shows the MSCI World Materials sub-industry weights as of December 31, 2007. We don't know what the sample portfolio weights should be, but we know it should add up to 100 percent. Of course, if managing against a broader benchmark, your Materials sector weight may add up to more or less than the Materials weight in the benchmark, depending on over- or underweight decisions.

Keeping the sub-industry weights in mind will help mitigate benchmark risk. If you have a portfolio of stocks with the same sub-industry

## Table 7.5   MSCI World Materials Sub-Industry Weights vs. Sample Portfolio

| Sub-Industry | MSCI World (%) | Sample Portfolio |
|---|---|---|
| Diversified Metals & Mining | 28.3 | ? |
| Steel | 14.0 | ? |
| Gold | 6.1 | ? |
| Aluminum | 2.4 | ? |
| Precious Metals & Minerals | 0.5 | ? |
| Commodity Chemicals | 2.5 | ? |
| Specialty Chemicals | 5.9 | ? |
| Diversified Chemicals | 15.3 | ? |
| Fertilizers & Agricultural Chemicals | 8.5 | ? |
| Industrial Gases | 5.1 | ? |
| Construction Materials | 5.2 | ? |
| Paper Products | 3.3 | ? |
| Forest Products | 1.0 | ? |
| Paper Packaging | 0.8 | ? |
| Metal & Glass Containers | 1.2 | ? |
| **Total** | 100.0 | 100.0% |

*Source:* Thomson Datastream; MSCI, Inc.[8] as of 12/31/07.

weights as the MSCI World Materials Index, you're *neutral*—taking no benchmark risk. However, if you feel strongly about a sub-industry, like Paper Packaging and decide to only purchase those firms (one of the smallest weights in the sector), you're taking a huge benchmark risk. The same is true if you significantly *underweight* a sub-industry. All the same rules apply as when you do this from a broader portfolio perspective, as we did earlier in this chapter.

The benchmark's sub-industry weights provide a jumping-off point in making further portfolio decisions. Once you make higher-level decisions on the sub-industries, you can make choices versus the benchmark by overweighting the sub-industries you feel likeliest to perform best and underweighting those likeliest to perform worst. Table 7.6 shows how you can make different portfolio bets against the benchmark by over- and underweighting sub-industries.

## Table 7.6   Portfolio A

| Sub-Industry | MSCI World (%) | Portfolio A (%) | Difference (%) |
|---|---|---|---|
| Diversified Metals & Mining | 28.3 | 37.0 | 8.7 |
| Steel | 14.0 | 21.0 | 7.0 |
| Gold | 6.1 | 9.0 | 2.9 |
| Aluminum | 2.4 | 0.0 | −2.4 |
| Precious Metals & Minerals | 0.5 | 0.0 | −0.5 |
| Commodity Chemicals | 2.5 | 0.0 | −2.5 |
| Specialty Chemicals | 5.9 | 9.0 | 3.1 |
| Diversified Chemicals | 15.3 | 7.0 | −8.3 |
| Fertilizers & Agricultural Chemicals | 8.5 | 11.0 | 2.5 |
| Industrial Gases | 5.1 | 5.0 | −0.1 |
| Construction Materials | 5.2 | 0.0 | −5.2 |
| Paper Products | 3.3 | 1.0 | −2.3 |
| Forest Products | 1.0 | 0.0 | −1.0 |
| Paper Packaging | 0.8 | 0.0 | −0.8 |
| Metal & Glass Containers | 1.2 | 0.0 | −1.2 |
| **Total** | 100.0 | 100.0 | 0 |

*Source:* Thomson Datastream; MSCI, Inc.[9] as of 12/31/07.

Note: Portfolio A might be a portfolio of all Materials stocks, or it can simply represent a neutral Materials sector allocation in a larger portfolio.

The "difference" column shows the relative difference between the benchmark and Portfolio A. In this example, Portfolio A is most overweight to Diversified Metals & Mining and Steel and most underweight to Diversified Chemicals and Construction Materials.

In other words, for this hypothetical example, Portfolio A's owner expects Diversified Metals & Mining and Steel to outperform the sector and Diversified Chemicals and Construction Materials to underperform the sector. But in terms of benchmark risk, Portfolio A remains fairly close to the benchmark weights, so its relative risk is quite modest. This is extremely important: By managing against a benchmark, you can make strategic choices to beat the index and are

## Table 7.7   Portfolio B

| Sub-Industry | MSCI World (%) | Portfolio B (%) | Difference (%) |
|---|---|---|---|
| Diversified Metals & Mining | 28.3 | 0.0 | −28.3 |
| Steel | 14.0 | 14.0 | 0.0 |
| Gold | 6.1 | 40.0 | 33.9 |
| Aluminum | 2.4 | 0.0 | −2.4 |
| Precious Metals & Minerals | 0.5 | 0.0 | −0.5 |
| Commodity Chemicals | 2.5 | 0.0 | −2.5 |
| Specialty Chemicals | 5.9 | 0.0 | −5.9 |
| Diversified Chemicals | 15.3 | 10.0 | −5.3 |
| Fertilizers & Agricultural Chemicals | 8.5 | 30.0 | 21.5 |
| Industrial Gases | 5.1 | 5.0 | −0.1 |
| Construction Materials | 5.2 | 1.0 | −4.2 |
| Paper Products | 3.3 | 0.0 | −3.3 |
| Forest Products | 1.0 | 0.0 | −1.0 |
| Paper Packaging | 0.8 | 0.0 | −0.8 |
| Metal & Glass Containers | 1.2 | 0.0 | −1.2 |
| **Total** | 100.0 | 100.0 | 0 |

Source: Thomson Datastream; MSCI, Inc.[10] as of 12/31/07.

well-diversified within the sector without concentrating too heavily in a specific area.

Table 7.7 is another example of relative portfolio weighting versus the benchmark. Portfolio B is significantly underweight to Diversified Metals & Mining and most overweight to Gold and Fertilizers & Agricultural Chemicals. Because the sub-industry weights are so different from the benchmark, Portfolio B takes on substantially more relative risk than Portfolio A.

Regardless of how your portfolio is positioned relative to the benchmark, it's important to use benchmarks to identify where your relative risks are before investing. Knowing the benchmark weights and having opinions on the future performance of each sub-industry is a crucial step in building a portfolio designed to beat the benchmark. Should you make the correct overweight and underweight decisions, you're likelier to beat the benchmark regardless of the individual securities held within. But even if you're wrong, you'll have diversified enough not to lose your shirt.

## Chapter Recap

A more effective approach to sector analysis is "top-down." A top-down investment methodology analyzes big picture factors such as economics, politics, and sentiment to forecast which investment categories are likely to outperform the market. A key part of the process is the use of benchmarks (such as the MSCI World Materials or S&P 500 Materials indexes), which are used as guidelines for building portfolios, monitoring performance, and managing risk. By analyzing portfolio drivers, we can identify which Materials industries and sub-industries are most attractive and unattractive, ultimately filtering down to stock selection.

- The top-down investment methodology first identifies and analyzes high-level portfolio drivers affecting broad categories of stocks. These drivers help determine portfolio country, sector, and style weights. The same methodology can be applied to a specific sector to determine industry and sub-industry weights.
- Quantitative factor screening helps narrow the list of potential portfolio holdings based on characteristics such as valuations, liquidity, and solvency.
- Stock selection is the last step in the top-down process. Stock selection attempts to find companies possessing strategic attributes consistent with higher-level portfolio drivers.
- Stock selection also attempts to find companies with the greatest probability of outperforming its peers.
- It's helpful to use a Materials benchmark as a guide when constructing a portfolio to determine your sub-industry overweights and underweights.

# 8

# SECURITY ANALYSIS

**N**ow that we've covered the top-down method, let's pick some stocks. This chapter walks you through analyzing individual Materials firms using the top-down method presented in Chapter 7. Specifically, we'll demonstrate a five-step process for analyzing firms relative to peers.

Every firm and every stock is different, and viewing them through the right lens is vital. Investors need a functional, consistent, and reusable framework for analyzing securities across the sector. While by no means comprehensive, the framework provided and the questions at this chapter's end should serve as good starting points to help identify strategic attributes and company-specific risks.

While volumes have been written about individual security analysis, a top-down investment approach de-emphasizes the importance of stock selection in a portfolio. As such, we'll talk about the basics of stock analysis for the beginner-to-intermediate investor. For a more thorough understanding of financial statement analysis, valuations, modeling, and other tools of security analysis, additional reading is suggested.

> ### Top-Down Recap
>
> As covered in Chapter 7, you can use the top-down method to make your biggest, most important portfolio decisions first. However, the same process applies when picking stocks, and those high-level portfolio decisions ultimately filter down to individual securities.
>
> Step one is analyzing the broader global economy and identifying various macro "drivers" affecting entire sectors or industries. Using the drivers, you can make general allocation decisions for countries, sectors, industries, and sub-industries versus the given benchmark. Step two is applying quantitative screening criteria to narrow the choice set of stocks. It's not until all those decisions are made that we get to analyze individual stocks. Security analysis is the third and final step.
>
> For the rest of the chapter, we assume you have already established a benchmark, solidified portfolio themes, made sub-industry overweight and underweight decisions, and are ready to analyze firms within a *peer group*. (A peer group is a group of stocks you'd generally expect to perform similarly because they operate in the same industry, possibly share the same geography, and have similar quantitative attributes.)

## MAKE YOUR SELECTION

Security analysis is nowhere near as complicated as it may seem—but that doesn't mean it's easy. Similar to your goal in choosing industry and sector weights, you've got one basic task: spot opportunities not currently discounted into prices. Or, put differently, know something others don't. Investors should analyze firms by taking consensus expectations for a company's estimated financial results and then assessing whether it will perform below, in line with, or above those baseline expectations. Profit opportunities arise when your expectations are different and more accurate than consensus expectations. Trading on widely known information or consensus expectations adds no value to the stock selection process. Doing so is really no different than trading on a coin flip.

The top-down method offers two ways to spot such opportunities. First, accurately predict high-level, macro themes affecting an industry or group of companies—these are your portfolio drivers. Second, find firms that will benefit *most* if those high-level themes and drivers play out. This is done by finding firms with *competitive advantages* (we'll explain this concept more in a bit).

Since the majority of excess return is added in higher-level decisions in the top-down process, it's not vital to pick the "best" stocks in the universe. Rather, you want to pick stocks with a good probability of outperforming their peers. Doing so can enhance returns without jeopardizing good top-down decisions by picking risky, go-big-or-go-home stocks. Being right more often than not should create outperformance relative to the benchmark over time.

## A FIVE-STEP PROCESS

Analyzing a stock against its peer group can be summarized as a five-step process:

1. Understand business and earnings drivers.
2. Identify strategic attributes.
3. Analyze fundamental and stock price performance.
4. Identify risks.
5. Analyze valuations and consensus expectations.

These five steps provide a consistent framework for analyzing firms in their peer groups. While these steps are far from a full stock analysis, they provide the basics necessary to begin making better stock selections.

### Step 1: Understand Business and Earnings Drivers

The first step is to understand what the business does, how it generates its earnings, and what drives those earnings. Here are a few tips to help in the process.

- **Industry overview:** Begin any analysis with a basic understanding of the firm's industry, including its drivers and risks. You should be familiar with how current economic trends affect the industry.
- **Company description:** Obtain a business description of the company, including an understanding of the products and services within each business segment. It's always best to go directly to a company's financial statements for this. (Almost every public firm makes their financial statements readily accessible online

these days.) Browse the firm's website and financial statements/ reports to gain an overview of the company and how it presents itself.

- **Corporate history:** Read the firm's history since its inception and over the last several years. An understanding of firm history may reveal its growth strategy or consistency with success and failure. It also will provide clues on what its true core competencies are. Ask questions like: Has it been an industry leader for decades, or is it a relative newcomer? Has it switched strategies or businesses often in the past?

- **Business segments:** Break down company revenues and earnings by business segment and geography to determine how and where it makes its money. Find out what drives results in each business and geographic segment. Begin thinking about how each of these business segments fits into your high-level themes.

- **Recent news/press releases:** Read all recently released news about the stock, including press releases. Do a Google search and see what comes up. Look for any significant announcements regarding company operations. What is the media's opinion of the firm? Is it a bellwether to the industry or a minor player?

- **Markets and customers:** Identify main customers and the markets it operates in. Determine whether the firm has any particularly large single customer or a concentrated customer base.

- **Competition:** Find the main competitors and how market share compares with other industry players. Is the industry highly segmented? Assess the industry's competitive landscape. Keep in mind the biggest competitors can sometimes lurk in different industries—sometimes even in different sectors! Get a feel for how the firm stacks up—is it an industry leader or a minor player? Does market share matter in that industry?

## Step 2: Identify Strategic Attributes

After gaining a firm grasp of firm operations, the next step is identifying strategic attributes consistent with higher-level portfolio themes. Also known as *competitive* or *comparative advantages*, strategic attributes are unique features allowing firms to outperform their industry or sector. Since industry peers are generally affected by the same high-level drivers, strong strategic attributes are the edge in creating superior performance. Examples of strategic attributes include:

- High relative market share
- Low-cost production
- Superior sales relationships/distribution
- Economic sensitivity
- Vertical integration
- Strong management/business strategy
- Geographic diversity or advantage
- Consolidator
- Strong balance sheet
- Niche market exposure
- Pure play
- Potential takeover target
- Proprietary technologies
- Strong brand name
- First mover advantage

### Strategic Attributes: Making Lemonade

How do strategic attributes help you analyze individual stocks? Consider a simple example: There are five lemonade stands of similar size, product, and quality within a city block. A scorching heat wave envelops the city, sending a rush of customers in search of lemonade. Which stand benefits most from the industry-wide surge in business? This likely depends on each stand's strategic attributes. Maybe one is a cost leader and has cheapest access to homegrown lemons. Maybe one has a geographic advantage and is located next to a basketball court full of thirsty players. Or maybe one has a superior business strategy with a "buy two, get one free" initiative that drives higher sales volume and a bigger customer base. Any of these are core strategic advantages.

Portfolio drivers help determine which kind of strategic attributes are likely to face head or tailwinds. After all, not all strategic attributes will benefit a firm in all environments. For example, while higher operating leverage might help a firm boost earnings when an industry is booming, it would have the opposite effect in a down cycle. A pertinent Materials example is access to iron ore reserves for a steel producer—an important strategic attribute from 2003–2007 due to the rising cost of raw materials. When iron ore prices decline, however, iron ore operations will create a drag on company earnings growth relative to other producers. Thus, it's essential to pick strategic attributes consistent with higher-level portfolio themes.

A strategic attribute is also only effective to the extent management recognizes and takes advantage of it. Execution is key. For example, if a firm's strategic attribute is technological expertise, it should focus its efforts on research and development to maintain that edge. If its strategic attribute is low-cost production relative to its peer group, it should capitalize by potentially lowering prices or expanding production (assuming the new production is also low cost) to gain market share.

Identifying strategic attributes may require thorough research of the firm's financial statements, website, news stories, history, and discussions with customers, suppliers, competitors, or management. Don't skimp on this step—be diligent and thorough in finding strategic attributes. It may feel an arduous task at times, but it's also among the most important in security selection.

## Step 3: Analyze Fundamentals and Stock Price Performance

Once you've gained a thorough understanding of the business, earnings drivers, and strategic attributes, the next step is analyzing firm performance both fundamentally and in the stock market.

Using the latest earnings releases and annual report, analyze company performance in recent quarters. Ask:

- What are recent revenue trends? Earnings? Margins? Which business segments are seeing rising or falling sales?

- Is the firm growing its business organically, because of acquisitions, or some other reason?
- How sustainable is their strategy?
- Are earnings growing because of strong demand or because of cost cutting?
- Are they using tax loopholes and one-time items?
- What is management's strategy to grow the business for the future?
- What is the financial health of the company?

Not all earnings results are created equal. Understanding what drives results gives clues to what will drive future performance.

Check the company's stock chart for the last few years and try to determine what has driven performance. Explain any big up or down moves and identify any significant news events. If the stock price has trended steadily downward despite consistently beating earnings estimates, there may be a force driving the whole industry downward, like expectations for lower metal prices. Likewise, if the company's stock soared despite reporting tepid earnings growth or prospects, there may be some force driving the industry higher, like takeover speculation. Or stocks can simply move in sympathy with the broader market. Whatever it is, make sure you know.

After reading the earnings calls of a firm and its peers (these are typically posted on the investor relations section of a firm's website every quarter and transcripts can also be found at http://seekingalpha.com/tag/transcripts), you'll begin to notice similar trends and events affecting the industry. Take note of these so you can distinguish between issues that are company-specific or industrywide. For example, economic growth or labor scarcity often affect entire Materials industries, but hedging policies or a government's tax policies may only affect specific producers.

## Step 4: Identify Risks

There are two main types of risks in security analysis: stock-specific risk and systematic risk (also known as non-stock specific risk). Both can be equally important to performance.

*Stock-specific risks*, as the name suggests, are issues affecting the company in isolation. These are mainly risks affecting a firm's business operations or future operations. Some company-specific risks are discussed in detail in the annual reports, 10-Ks for US firms and the 20-Fs for foreign filers (found at www.sec.gov). But one can't rely solely on firms' self-identifying risk factors. You must see what analysts are saying about them and identify all risks for yourself. Some examples include:

- Stock ownership concentration (insider or institutional)
- Customer concentration
- Sole suppliers
- Excessive leverage or lack of access to financing
- Obsolete products
- Poor operational track record
- High cost of products versus competitors
- Late Securities and Exchange Commission (SEC) filings
- Qualified audit opinions
- Hedging activities
- Pension or benefit underfunding risk
- Regulatory or legal (pending litigation)
- Pending corporate actions
- Executive departures
- Regional, political/governmental risk

*Systematic risks* include macroeconomic or geopolitical events out of a company's control. While the risks may affect a broad set of firms, they will have varying effects on each. Some examples include:

- Commodity prices
- Industry cost inflation
- Economic activity
- Labor scarcity
- Strained supply chain
- Legislation affecting taxes, royalties, or subsidies
- Geopolitical risks

- Capital expenditures
- Interest rates
- Currency
- Weather

Identifying stock-specific risks helps an investor evaluate the relative risk and reward potential of firms within a peer group. Identifying systematic risks helps you make informed decisions about which sub-industries and countries to overweight or underweight.

If you don't feel strongly about any company in a peer group within a sub-industry you wish to overweight, you could pick the company with the least stock-specific risk. This would help to achieve the goal of picking firms with the greatest probability of outperforming its peer group and still perform in line with your higher-level themes and drivers.

## Step 5: Analyze Valuations and Consensus Expectations

Valuations can be tricky. They *are* tools used to evaluate market sentiment and expectations for firms. They *are not* a foolproof way to see if a stock is "cheap" or "expensive." Valuations are primarily used to compare firms against their peer group (or peer average) or a company's valuation relative to its own history. As mentioned earlier, stocks move not on the expected, but the unexpected. We aim to try and gauge what the consensus expects for a company's future performance and then assess whether that company will perform below, in line, or above expectations.

Valuations provide little information by themselves in predicting future stock performance. Just because one company's P/E is 20 while another's is 10 doesn't mean you should buy the one at 10 because it's "cheaper." There's likely a reason why one company has a different valuation than another, including such things as strategic attributes, earnings expectations, sentiment, stock-specific risks, and management's reputation. The main usefulness of valuations is explaining why a company's valuation differs from its peers and determining if it's justified.

There are many different valuation metrics investors use in security analysis. Some of the most popular include:

- P/E—price-to-earnings
- P/FE—price-to-forward earnings
- P/B—price-to-book
- P/S—price-to-sales
- P/CF—price-to-cash-flow
- DY—dividend yield
- EV/EBITDA—enterprise value to earnings before interest, taxes, depreciation, and amortization

Once you've compiled the valuations for a peer group, try to estimate why there are relative differences and if they're justified. Is a company's relatively low valuation due to stock-specific risk or low confidence from investors? Is the company's forward P/E relatively high because consensus is wildly optimistic about the stock? A firm's higher valuation may be entirely justified, for example, if it has a growth rate greater than its peers. A lower valuation may be warranted for a company facing a challenging operating environment in which it is losing market share. Seeing valuations in this way will help to differentiate firms and spot potential opportunities or risks.

Valuations should be used in combination with previous analysis of a company's fundamentals, strategic attributes, and risks. For example, the following grid shows how an investor could combine an analysis of strategic attributions and valuations to help pick firms.

Stocks with relatively low valuations but attractive strategic attributes may be underappreciated by the market. Stocks with relatively high valuations but no discernible strategic attributes may be overvalued by the market. Either way, use valuations appropriately and in the context of a larger investment opinion about a stock, not as a panacea for true value.

|  |  | Valuation Low | Valuation High |
|---|---|---|---|
| Strategic Attributes | Relatively Attractive | Best |  |
|  | Relatively Unattractive |  | Worst |

## IMPORTANT QUESTIONS TO ASK

While this chapter's framework can be used to analyze any firm, there are additional factors specific to the Materials sector that must be considered. The following section provides some of the most important factors and questions to consider when researching firms in the sector. Answers to these questions should help distinguish between firms within a peer group and help identify strategic attributes and stock-specific risks. While there are countless other questions and factors that could and should be asked when researching Materials firms, these should serve as a good starting point.

**Supply/Demand Environment:** For globally priced goods, what is the product's supply/demand environment around the world? And for regionally priced goods, what is it within the firm's countries of operation? Have prices recently been affected by changes or expectations of changes in the supply/demand equation? Both supply and demand side factors will have a great influence on prices, which can be volatile.

**Revenues and Earnings Breakdown:** Most firms produce more than a single product. The more diversified the revenue, the less exposed the firm is to fluctuations in a single product or end market. Its product mix will also determine what has the greatest effect on the firm's future earnings and performance. How are the firm's revenues and earnings divided between products? How does this compare to competitors? Is it more concentrated or diversified?

**Production Growth:** What is the firm's production growth history? Is the firm consistently growing production or is it experiencing declines? What is its production growth relative to peers? What is its strategy for increasing production? Is it organic or through acquisitions?

Organic growth carries operational risk and could potentially yield limited success due to unexpected obstacles and higher costs, difficult governmental royalties, or regulatory negotiations.

Growth through acquisitions, however, could increase integration risks and raises the possibility of paying too much for a firm or asset.

Of course, production growth for the sake of production growth is not always a good thing. If done on a large enough scale, it may depress prices and actually reduce total earnings. Instead, firms may find share buybacks or dividends as better means of increasing shareholder value.

**Reserve Replacement:** This is most applicable to industries where production is limited by available resources. This includes producers in metals and mining, construction materials, lumber, and some segments of chemicals such as mined fertilizers. What is the firm's history of reserve replacement? Does it have a strategy in place to grow reserves? How many years can it sustain production with current reserves? Firms with relatively long life reserves may not need to take major risks to grow production in the future. This could be a distinct competitive advantage.

**Hedging:** To what degree does the firm use hedging in its operations? How exposed are the firm's operations to changes in prices of input costs and its end product? Materials firms' hedging strategies show which ones have the most upside and downside relative to rising or falling prices and raw material input costs.

**Geographic Breakdown & Geopolitical Risk:** Regional prices and volumes demanded can vary dramatically between home and export markets. Thus, regional diversification can mitigate risks of big changes in any one market. For globally priced goods, a breakdown of regional production will help identify political and social risks to production, while a breakdown of regional consumption will identify the primary drivers.

Where are most of the firm's current and future planned production sites? Are they in politically stable or unstable countries? What percentage of production comes from politically unstable regions? Do they have a solid history of operating in foreign territories? Has the company historically had good or troubled relations with governments in the region? Are labor unions historically strong or weak in those regions? Do tariffs, subsidies, or price caps exist? Is the firm beholden to trade problems with other regions? For regionally priced goods, how quickly is the product's end market growing in its regions of operation?

While a firm with relatively high exposure to a geopolitically unstable region may face higher risks of government intervention or production disruption, the potential additions to production growth may warrant these risks and are not always inherent negatives.

**Production Costs:** Even firms in the same industry can have highly different cost profiles. What factors are driving its production costs? What are the firm's production costs relative to its peers? What is the firm's strategy to mitigate industry cost inflation? Does its plan differ from competitors? If it's a low-cost producer compared to peers, does it have a strategy to take advantage of that? If it's a high-cost producer, does it have a strategy to change that?

**Vertical Integration:** Does the firm benefit from some degree of vertical integration? (That is, does it have the ability to handle multiple stages of the production process by itself?) To what degree is it reliant on other firms in its operations? Firms with more vertical integration may be able to mitigate cost increases in times of industry cost inflation.

**Transportation:** Transportation costs are particularly important for bulk goods (with lower value-to-weight ratios) where transportation makes up a greater percentage of overall costs. How does it deliver its product to consumers? How far away are its consumers? What impact will rising or falling transportation costs have on it compared to competitors? (Ocean freight rates can be found through the Baltic Dry Index—covered in Chapter 5.) Are there any transportation bottlenecks, and if so, does it have a plan to address them? How has the firm responded to such bottlenecks in the past?

**Government Control:** Are the firm's shares owned or controlled by a government, and if so, to what degree? Does the government play an active role in firm decisions and policies, and if so, has it ever made decisions in conflict with the interests of shareholders? Does the firm secure free market pricing for its product or does the government set them? Has the company historically been given special treatment or favored over other producers for contracts, loans, or taxes?

Governments in emerging markets will likely play a bigger and more volatile role in the development of their country's natural resources than in developed ones. Government-controlled firms may be subject to unique taxes, royalties, subsidies, or price controls. Dividend policies may also be set in the best interest of balancing budgets rather than future earnings. Depending on the circumstances, government ownership can work for or against a company, but you'll want to know its impact.

**Legislative Risks:** Are there any legislative risks? These can include royalties, windfall taxes, environmental legislation, price caps, labor laws, subsidies, tariffs, and the nationalization of assets. Emission laws in particular are a popular topic of debate in the developed world.

**Competition and Barriers to Entry:** What is the competitive landscape of the firm's peers? Does it compete against government-owned firms (which have historically received special treatment)? Does the firm operate in a region or industry with significant barriers to entry? Barriers to entry may include dominant market share, capital intensity, patents, proprietary technology, a concentrated industry, and difficulty in obtaining regulatory or environmental permits. High barriers to entry typically provide pricing power and reduce competition.

**Technology and Innovation:** In the Materials sector, this trait primarily applies to chemical producers. New technology and innovation related to new chemicals and the creation of new end markets for existing chemicals can be incredibly important in the chemical industry. Does the firm possess any proprietary technologies or patents giving it a competitive edge? Does it have a history of innovation? Is its end market dynamic, requiring the consistent release of new products, or do they specialize in more mature markets?

**Brand Names:** Again, within the Materials sector, this trait primarily applies to the chemical industry. Brand names provide pricing power. Does the firm have any brand names? How much higher are they able to price their product than competitors?

**Regulation:** How are the firm's operations affected by regulation? Does the firm currently operate in a favorable regulatory environment? How might that change? What is the firm's history with gaining regulatory approval for its products (primarily applicable to genetically modified seed producers) or operations by country? Firms with highly regulated assets are exposed to regulatory risks, but they may also have more stable returns.

**Market Share:** Dominant market share often provides greater pricing power, especially for regionally priced goods. What is the firm's market share in each of its business segments? How fragmented are the consumers in its end market? Does the firm have pricing power for its products and services? For regionally priced products, how do their prices and raw material costs compare to competitors?

**Margins:** Are margins growing or shrinking? Has the company historically offset higher costs with higher prices? How does its margins compare to peers? High margins in a vacuum tell you little since some industries historically hold higher margins than others, and it's usually well-known and taken into account in share prices.

Margins are particularly important to consider for chemical producers. Strong economic growth not only bolsters the chemical industry, but can also help prop up the price of oil and natural gas, which are its main inputs. Therefore, its ability to pass on costs through higher prices can be a key attribute in an environment of rising raw material prices. The more cyclical and commoditized its end market, the less pricing power it typically controls.

Margins are particularly important to consider for chemical producers. Strong economic growth not only bolsters the chemical industry, but can also help prop up the price of oil and natural gas, which are its main inputs. Therefore, its ability to pass on costs through higher prices can be a key attribute in an environment of rising raw material prices. The more cyclical and commoditized its end market, the less pricing power it typically controls.

**Cash Flow Use:** How is the firm spending its cash flow? To what degree is it buying back shares, paying dividends, spending on capital expenditures, or paying down debt? Depending on industry conditions, investors may prefer a firm rewarding shareholders with dividends and share buybacks over one taking on risky new production plans.

**Balance Sheet:** Many firms carry heavy debt loads due to their capital-intensive nature, so financial health can vary widely. Those with greater financial resources could be more capable of funding future growth opportunities. Does the firm have the financial ability to make large acquisitions to fuel growth? Does the firm's balance sheet allow it to take on additional leverage?

Debt isn't necessarily a bad thing—many firms generate an excellent return on borrowed funds. In either case, it's vital to understand the capital structure of a firm.

**Interest Rates:** How sensitive is the firm's operations to interest rates? Are rising or falling rates good or bad for the firm's operations and share price? Firms with greater leverage tend to be more affected by interest rate movements due to changes in interest expense.

**Chapter Recap**

Security analysis is not nearly as complicated as it seems. In the top-down investment process, stocks are essentially tools we use to take advantage of opportunities we identify in higher-level themes. Once an attractive segment of the market is identified, we attempt to determine the firms most likely to outperform their peers by finding firms with strategic attributes. While the five-step security selection process is just one of many ways to research firms, it is an effective framework for selecting securities within the top-down process.

Do not limit yourself to the questions provided in this chapter when researching Materials firms—they are just some tools to help you distinguish between firms. The more questions you ask, the better your analysis will be.

- Stock selection, the third and final step in the top-down investment process, attempts to identify securities that will benefit from our high-level portfolio themes.
- Ultimately, stock selection attempts to spot opportunities not currently discounted into prices.
- To identify firms most likely to outperform their peer group, we must find firms that possess competitive advantages (a.k.a strategic attributes).
- A five-step security selection process can be used as a framework to research firms.
- Firms within each industry have specific characteristics and strategies separating potential winners from losers. Asking the right questions can help identify those features.

# 9

# MATERIALIZE YOUR PORTFOLIO

## Investing Strategies

In this chapter, we'll discuss various Materials investment strategies, including examples of how to invest throughout a market cycle. We'll also briefly cover investing directly in underlying commodities. The strategies include:

- Adding value at the industry and sub-industry level
- Adding value at the security level
- Adding value in a Materials sector downturn
- Investing in commodities

While the strategies presented here are by no means comprehensive, they provide a good starting point for constructing a portfolio that can increase your likelihood of outperforming a Materials benchmark. They should also help spur some investment strategy ideas of your own. After all, using this framework to discover information few others have yet to discover is what investing is all about.

## STRATEGY 1: ADDING VALUE AT THE INDUSTRY AND SUB-INDUSTRY LEVEL

The first strategy is overweighting and underweighting Materials industries or sub-industries based on your market outlook and analysis (e.g., the top-down method). Within the Materials sector, each industry and sub-industry falls in and out of favor frequently—no one area outperforms consistently over the long term. Each will lead or lag depending on drivers like the direction of raw material prices, production costs, the regulatory environment, and global or regional growth in end markets.

A look at the performance of the MSCI All Country World Materials industries from 1995 to 2007 (Table 9.1) illustrates the variability of returns. Calendar year industry total returns are compared to the Materials sector total returns. Shaded regions highlight industry outperformance.

The fundamentals, themes, and drivers covered in this book can be seen throughout the time period. Notably:

1. Metals & Mining outperformed from 2003 to 2007 when the industrialization of the emerging markets accelerated, infrastructure construction surged, and global per capita GDP rapidly increased. It also was the most volatile industry.
2. Chemicals' largest period of outperformance came during the late 1990s in a period of strong economic growth and low oil prices. It also was the least volatile industry.
3. Construction Materials produced strong returns from 2003 to 2006 when global construction surged, due to booming residential housing markets in the developed world and infrastructure build outs in the emerging markets.
4. Containers & Packaging's strongest period of returns involved the end of the bear market of 2000 to 2002, helped by its defensive nature, with the majority of the industry servicing the relatively inelastic food and beverage markets.

Ultimately, your decision to overweight or underweight a sub-industry relative to the benchmark should jive with your high-level

**Table 9.1  MSCI All Country World Materials Industry Total Returns**

| | Materials Sector (%) | Metals & Mining (%) | Chemicals (%) | Construction Materials (%) | Paper & Forestry (%) | Containers & Packaging (%) |
|---|---|---|---|---|---|---|
| 1995 | 3.7 | 0.2 | 11.7 | -3.6 | -2.0 | -2.1 |
| 1996 | 5.5 | -2.2 | 16.2 | 0.3 | 2.5 | -3.8 |
| 1997 | -11.0 | -25.9 | 0.9 | -9.0 | -7.1 | -13.7 |
| 1998 | -3.0 | -12.4 | 1.3 | 9.1 | -3.5 | -8.5 |
| 1999 | 34.0 | 58.7 | 21.3 | 24.5 | 40.9 | 12.6 |
| 2000 | -15.2 | -20.1 | -8.2 | -18.9 | -18.9 | -27.9 |
| 2001 | -2.9 | 5.7 | -12.0 | 3.4 | 1.8 | 2.6 |
| 2002 | -1.2 | 3.0 | -1.8 | -11.6 | -6.8 | 19.5 |
| 2003 | 48.2 | 67.8 | 35.4 | 53.1 | 34.0 | 32.8 |
| 2004 | 18.7 | 16.5 | 21.1 | 31.6 | 8.9 | 11.8 |
| 2005 | 21.1 | 36.8 | 13.0 | 23.8 | -7.1 | -5.2 |
| 2006 | 31.3 | 41.0 | 21.1 | 37.5 | 19.5 | 12.3 |
| 2007 | 38.7 | 50.5 | 37.6 | 6.3 | -1.5 | 6.6 |
| **Average Ann. Return** | 11.2 | 13.1 | 11.1 | 9.4 | 3.5 | 1.7 |
| **Cumulative Return** | *299.4* | *398.2* | *294.4* | *223.3* | *55.8* | *24.9* |
| **Standard Deviation** | 17.6 | 22.9 | 15.7 | 17.4 | 20.0 | 18.6 |

*Source:* Thomson Datastream; MSCI, Inc.[1] 12/31/1994–12/31/2007.

portfolio drivers. Based on the themes and drivers covered throughout this book, you should now have an understanding of the fundamentals driving stock market returns and the tools to track them
moving forward. Note: *Always remember past performance is no guar-
antee of future performance.* No set of rules works for all time, and you
should always analyze the entire situation before investing—starting
with expectations of how supply and demand may shift. The past is
about understanding context and precedent for investing—it's not a
road map for the future.

## How to Implement Sub-Asset Allocation Over- and Underweights

Once you've evaluated a sector's fundamentals and formed opinions
about expected returns, follow these two steps to implement industry
or sub-industry allocation over- and underweights:

1. Determine the weight relative to your benchmark's weight
   in that category. The size of your relative bet should be pro-
   portional to your conviction. When you have only mild
   conviction, make a modest bet against the benchmark. When
   you believe you have significant information others don't have,
   make a bigger bet. But never make a bet so large that, if you're
   wrong, will inflict irreparable damage to your portfolio's return
   versus the benchmark.

2. Determine how you plan to fill out the allocation. You have
   several alternatives. You might simply buy all the stocks in that
   category if you don't feel you have any useful security-specific
   insights. You might buy some representative stocks, perhaps
   either the biggest or those with the highest correlation to the
   category. You might buy an exchange-traded fund (ETF) or
   mutual fund that encompasses the category. (For more information on available ETFs, visit www.ishares.com, www.sectorspdr
   .com, or www.masterdata.com.) Or you might try to add additional value with security selection strategies.

## Industry and Sub-Industry Cheat Sheet

Sectors and their components are dynamic, and fundamentals change over time. For reference, however, here's a quick cheat sheet with pointers on each industry and sub-industry.

# METALS & MINING

- The industry can be thought of as the "high beta" industry in Materials. It tends to be extremely cyclical and volatile due to its extreme levels of capital intensity and operating leverage.
- It often outperforms the rest of the sector when raw material prices are rising, due to strong economic growth and rising global GDP per capita (industrialization).
- In recent years, Metals & Mining was particularly sensitive to economic growth in the emerging markets, where most new metal consumption took place.

## Diversified Metals & Mining

- Makes up a large weight in most major Materials indexes, so it's a good idea to hold at least a small allocation of it in any Materials portfolio to reduce benchmark risk.
- This sub-industry is extremely capital intensive, tends to be dominated by large producers, is highly cyclical, and outperforms when raw materials prices are rising.
- Benefits from strong economic growth and periods of industrialization when global GDP per capita is rapidly rising.

## Gold

- Often outperforms other Materials sub-industries in periods of uncertainty when investors are looking for a safe haven or are fearful of inflation.

## Aluminum

- Its demand drivers are very similar to Diversified Metals & Mining.
- Because it's the most energy-intensive metal to produce, it often outperforms in periods of strong economic growth and falling energy prices.
- Performance between producers in this sub-industry may differ significantly depending on the direction in energy prices and access to lower or higher cost energy resources.

*(Continued)*

## Steel

- Steel producers benefit from many of the same factors as Diversified Metals & Mining, although the industry is less capital intensive, which reduces barriers to entry and makes supply more volatile.
- It should be evaluated regionally. Important comparison factors include: iron-ore versus scrap-based producers, bar versus flat steel producers, and vertically integrated versus non-vertically integrated production models.
- It often underperforms miners in periods of rising raw material costs, although regional exceptions are common.
- Vertically integrated producers with upstream raw material operations often outperform non-vertically integrated producers in periods of rising raw material prices. In such periods, firms with upstream iron ore operations also generally outperform firms with upstream scrap recycling operations, due to a higher fixed cost structure and greater operating leverage.
- It's a fragmented sub-industry of small producers and therefore generally benefits when small cap outperforms relative to large cap.

## Precious Metals & Minerals

- It benefits from many of the same drivers as Gold, but is a very small sub-industry. Unless you have a very strong opinion, you usually don't want to hold a significant weight in it due to benchmark risk.

## CHEMICALS

- Most of the industry is an intermediary on the way from oil or natural gas to a finished product, and broad economic growth is the only driver big enough to move all the thousands of end products in the same direction at the same time.
- The industry often outperforms in periods of strong economic growth and stable or falling energy prices.
- The industry has higher variable costs and lower operating leverage than the mining industry (it must keep buying its raw material versus paying only once for the land). This makes Chemicals less cyclical with smaller booms and busts.

## Commodity Chemicals

- Often outperforms in periods of strong economic growth and stagnant or falling oil prices.

- The sub-industry is characterized by large, highly cyclical firms competing primarily on efficiencies and production costs. Therefore, they hold very little pricing power and rely on economic growth as a driver.

## Specialty Chemicals

- Must be evaluated regionally and according to specialized products created for niche markets.
- As with commodity chemicals, specialties are sensitive to economic growth and benefit from lower energy prices. With so many diverse end markets, however, you should choose your firms carefully as they may experience wide divergences in performance.
- Given the regional and niche markets, competition is generally the lightest in this industry, which helps specialty chemical firms retain some of the greatest pricing power within the industry. This makes the sub-industry among the most resistant Materials sub-industries to economic downturns.

## Diversified Chemicals

- It is generally filled with larger conglomerates that either don't fit neatly into other chemical sub-industries or are vertically integrated with both commodity and specialty chemical arms.
- The same tips from the commodity and specialty chemical sub-industries apply. In this case you may simply need to mix your understanding of both sub-industries to determine your ultimate expectations.

## Fertilizers & Agricultural Chemicals

- It is heavily influenced by government intervention. This includes tariffs, subsidies, trade restrictions, government stockpiles, and biofuel mandates. Caution should always be used when trying to predict government actions since political sentiment can be fickle.
- Most of the firms can be evaluated as specialty chemical producers. Genetically modified seed producers, however, have many traits in common with technology firms, while potash and phosphate miners have many traits in common with mining firms. Due to higher operating leverage and greater barriers to entry, fertilizer miners often outperform processors in periods of rising fertilizer prices.

*(Continued)*

## Industrial Gases

- Industrial gases should be evaluated regionally. The sub-industry primarily benefits from strong economic growth and rising levels of manufacturing, oil exploration, and oil processing.

## CONSTRUCTION MATERIALS

- It is extremely sensitive to total construction expenditures and often benefits during periods of rising construction growth.
- The industry should be evaluated regionally due to its extremely low value-to-weight ratio and limited ability to be profitably shipped. Construction aggregate is generally never shipped long distances, but some trade in cement does take place.
- Construction aggregate producers are more sensitive to non-residential construction, and cement producers are more sensitive to residential construction.
- Global production is concentrated in a small group of dominant conglomerates producing cement and construction aggregate. In the US, however, distinctive cement and construction aggregate firms exist.

## PAPER & FOREST PRODUCTS

- A small industry, dominated by its paper component in most benchmarks. See Paper Products for primary drivers.
- Unless you have great conviction in your beliefs, it's unlikely you'll want to hold a significant weight due to benchmark risk.

### Paper Products

- End markets are primarily in the developed world, while much of the end markets for other Materials sub-industries are in emerging markets. Therefore, it often outperforms during periods when the economic growth rate in the developed world is increasing relative to the economic growth rate in emerging markets.

### Forest Products

- The sub-industry is primarily driven by regional residential construction.

## CONTAINERS & PACKAGING

- Often acts defensively with primary end markets in the relatively inelastic end markets of food and beverages.
- Rising raw material prices are a negative due to primary inputs of metal, plastics, and paper.
- Firms primarily compete on operating costs and distribution networks.
- Firms focused on food and beverage end markets are typically the least cyclical, and firms focused on packaging for shipping are the most cyclical within the industry.
- Unless you have great conviction in your beliefs, it is unlikely you'll want to hold a significant weight due to benchmark risk.

### Metal & Glass Containers

- Often acts as a defensive sub-industry.
- See Containers & Packaging for drivers.

### Paper Packaging

- Often acts as a defensive sub-industry.
- See Containers & Packaging for drivers.

## STRATEGY 2: ADDING VALUE AT THE SECURITY LEVEL

A more advanced strategy entails investing in firms within a sub-industry based on a specific business mix. This strategy could be based on different opinions about specific basic materials, input costs, end markets, regions, or some combination of all the above. For example, if you think copper prices will rise while iron ore prices will fall in the near future, you could:

- Buy copper firms and sell short iron ore firms.
- Buy copper firms with little to no hedging relative to peers.
- Buy iron ore firms with relatively greater iron ore hedges than peers.

- Own non-vertically integrated steel firms and avoid or sell short vertically integrated firms.
- Own iron ore–based steel producers and avoid or sell short scrap-based producers.

These are just a few examples. Countless other tactics could be employed within sub-industries. As you become more familiar with specific Materials firms and their industries, you can eventually develop your own strategies. Always be vigilant for company-specific issues that could cause a stock to act differently than you would expect in the context of your broader strategy. (And be sure to revisit Chapter 8 for how to select individual stocks.)

## STRATEGY 3: ADDING VALUE IN A MATERIALS SECTOR DOWNTURN

Most of this book focused on what drives the Materials sector and its industries forward. But what could cause a Materials boom to bust? No one sector or industry can outperform forever. The stock market eventually sniffs out all opportunities for excess returns and sector leadership changes. So it's important to review all the drivers and question your high-level portfolio themes regularly.

One obvious trigger for a Materials sector downturn would be a decline in basic materials commodity prices. While there are countless reasons why this could happen, here are a few examples to consider.

### Falling Demand

- Recession—regional or global; perceived or real
- Prolonged high prices
- Increased substitution
- Increased recycling

### Increasing Supply

- New mines or processing plants beginning production
- Increased output from existing mines and processing plants

- New technology increasing production rates
- Increasing global inventories
- Easing geopolitical uncertainty
- Free trade policies
- Legislation

Should your analysis lead you to believe the next 12 months will be a bad time for Materials stocks—because of the reasons above or something else—then it may be appropriate to either reduce or eliminate your weight in Materials firms or adopt a defensive position in the portfolio.

### How to Implement Your Strategy

If you have lower or negative expectations for the sector, you can:

- Get underweight by selling Materials stocks you already own.
- Short individual securities or Materials ETFs in an attempt to capitalize on an expected decline.
- Purchase inverse ETFs such as the UltraShort Basic Materials Proshares (ticker: SMN). These should rise in price if Materials stocks in general fall.
- Purchase put options on Materials stocks or indexes.
- Short commodities futures (see Strategy 4).

Because of the potential leverage involved, strategies involving options (which can be used either to augment an over- or underweight) and margin should *only* be used by sophisticated investors. Shorting is also a more sophisticated strategy. Keep in mind, significantly deviating from your benchmark involves the significant risk of missing equity-like upside should you be wrong. Significant deviations from your benchmark should only take place when you have strong convictions that you know something others do not.

## STRATEGY 4: INVESTING IN COMMODITIES

One of the most direct ways to invest in basic materials is commodity speculation. Why mess with pesky stocks when you're most interested in price movements of the underlying materials? Investing directly in gold, copper, platinum, lumber, or numerous other basic materials is the most direct way to gain exposure to changes in their prices. Just because gold prices rise or fall doesn't necessarily mean gold stocks will do the same. As covered in Chapter 3, though commodity prices typically have the greatest impact on Materials company earnings, factors like costs, production growth, and government regulations can cause producers' performance to differ significantly from the underlying commodity. Commodity investing gets right to the heart of the matter.

But caution: Directly buying commodities is a very different process than buying stocks. It involves different tools and analyses not covered in this book. Commodity investing is also not for everyone. Commodity prices can be extremely volatile, moving rapidly on unpredictable events. Significant leverage is also commonly used in commodity investing. Fortunes have been made and lost in mere days by speculating on commodities. Investors planning to invest in commodities should be prepared to stomach extreme volatility and have high risk tolerance. That's the dark side of commodity investing.

Commodities can also be used as a hedge. If you expect commodities to decline significantly in the short- to medium-term but still want to hold your material stocks for the long-term, you could short commodities in the futures market or use options to bet against prices. This too entails higher risk if not structured properly and should only be attempted by sophisticated investors.

## How to Implement Your Strategy

The most direct way to invest directly in commodities is to call your custodian or broker and set up a futures account, which allows you to invest directly in commodity futures. There are also several ways to buy securities tied to the price of some basic materials without a futures account through other investment vehicles like ETFs or mutual funds. Table 9.2 outlines a variety of ETFs and ETNs (exchange-traded notes) designed to track commodity prices. Note: These are just a few examples of securities linked to the price of

## Table 9.2   Commodity Tracking ETFs and ETNs

| Name | Ticker | Commodity |
|------|--------|-----------|
| Ishares COMEX Gold Trust | IAU | Gold |
| SPDR Gold Trust | GLD | Gold |
| Ishares Silver Trust | SLV | Silver |
| IPath AIG Industrial Metal ETN | JJM | Industrial Metals |
| PowerShares DB Base Metals Fund | DBB | Base Metals (Non-Iron Industrial Metals) |
| IPath AIG Copper ETN | JJC | Copper |
| IPath AIG Nickel ETN | JJN | Nickel |
| DB Gold Short ETN | DGZ | Inverse Gold |
| DB Double Short Gold ETN | DZZ | Double Inverse Gold |

basic materials. Further research should be done for more investment options through sites such as www.ishares.com, www.sectorspdr.com, and www.masterdata.com.

Because commodity investing is not the focus of this book, we won't go into further detail, but there are many publications available for more information about investing directly in commodities.

We've covered a lot in these pages—Materials' basics, drivers, and commonly watched industry fundamentals. But remember—like all sectors, Materials is dynamic. The drivers and fundamentals vital today may not be tomorrow. But with the top-down method, you can apply a consistent framework to analyze the sector regardless of the current environment.

## Chapter Recap

We couldn't possibly list every investment strategy out there for this dynamic sector. Different strategies will work best at different times. Some will become obsolete. New ones will be discovered. Whatever strategies you choose, *always know you could be wrong!* Decisions to significantly overweight or underweight a sub-industry relative to the benchmark, using shorting or

*(Continued)*

options strategies, or speculating on commodity prices should be based on a multitude of factors, including an assessment of risk. The point of benchmarking is to properly diversify, so make sure you always have counterstrategies built into your portfolio.

- There are numerous ways to invest in the Materials sector. These include investing directly in commodities, utilizing indexes or mutual funds, or buying the stocks themselves.
- Investors can enhance returns by overweighting and underweighting Materials sub-industries based on a variety of high-level drivers. For example, Diversified Metals & Mining tends to outperform Chemicals during periods of rising raw material prices.
- An advanced strategy involves making bets on firms with different business lines within sub-industries, like buying a Diversified Metals & Mining company that produces copper and shorting another that produces steel.
- Trading the commodities directly offers the best way to speculate directly on the movement of raw material prices. However, commodities can be highly volatile, and analysis involves different tools and strategies than those required for stocks.

# Appendix A
# Materials Sector Resources

While by no means exhaustive, the following is a list of websites and publications that may be helpful in following economic events, sector-specific statistics, and news throughout the Materials sector. While not specifically focused on the Materials sector, you can also find Fisher Investments' up-to-date views on broader markets and the economy at www.marketminder.com.

## ECONOMIC SOURCES

- US Census Bureau (www.census.gov)
- US Bureau of Economic Analysis (www.bea.gov)
- Statistical Office of the European Communities (Eurostat) (epp.eurostat.ec.europa.eu)
- International Monetary Fund (IMF) (www.imf.org)
- Organisation for Economic Cooperation and Development (OECD) (www.oecd.org)
- World Bank (www.worldbank.org)
- US Department of Agriculture (www.usda.gov)
- World Trade Organization (WTO) (www.wto.org)

## MATERIALS SECTOR SOURCES

- US Geological Survey (minerals.usgs.gov/minerals/pubs/commodity/)

- London Metal Exchange (www.lme.co.uk)
- New York Mercantile Exchange (www.nymex.com)
- Institute of Scrap Recycling (www.isri.org)
- World Mine Cost Data Exchange (www.minecost.com)
- Virtual Metals Group (www.virtualmetals.co.uk)
- Platts (www.platts.com/Metals/Resources)
- Metal Bulletin (www1.metalbulletin.com)
- Minerals UK (www.bgs.ac.uk/mineralsuk/home.html)
- Mineral Information Institute
  (www.mii.org/commonminerals.html)
- National Mining Association (www.nma.org)
- Mine Web (www.mineweb.com)

## MATERIALS INDUSTRY & SUB-INDUSTRY SOURCES

- Steel
  - International Iron & Steel Institute (www.worldsteel.org)
  - American Iron & Steel Institute (www.steel.org)
  - SteelGuru (www.steelguru.com)
  - World Steel Dynamics (www.worldsteeldynamics.com)
  - The Tex Report (www.texreport.co.jp/xenglish)
  - Steel Business Briefing (www.steelbb.com)
- Copper
  - International Copper Study Group (www.icsg.org)
  - Copper Development Association (www.copper.org)
- Nickel
  - International Nickel Study Group (www.insg.org)
  - Nickel Institute (www.nickelinstitute.org)
- Lead & Zinc
  - International Lead & Zinc Study Group (www.ilzsg.org)
  - International Zinc Association (www.iza.com)
- Gold
  - World Gold Council (www.gold.org)
  - Gold Fields Mineral Services (GFMS) (www.gfms.co.uk)
  - GOLDSHEET Mining Directory
    (www.goldsheetlinks.com/production.htm)

- Silver
  - Silver Institute (www.silverinstitute.org)
- Coal
  - World Coal Institute (www.worldcoal.org)
  - US Energy Information Administration (www.eia.doe.gov)
- Aluminum
  - Aluminum Association (www.aluminum.org)
- Chemicals
  - Chemical Market Associates, Inc. (www.cmaiglobal.com)
- Fertilizers
  - International Fertilizer Industry Association (www.fertilizer.org)
- Industrial Gases
  - Gas World (www.gasworld.com)
- Cement & Construction Aggregate
  - Portland Cement Association (www.cement.org)
  - Portland Cement Association Economic Research (www.cement.org/econ/index.asp)
- Paper & Lumber
  - American Forest & Paper Association (www.afandpa.org)
- Containers & Packaging
  - Packaging Today (www.packagingtoday.com)

# Appendix B
# Top 10 Materials Firms by Industry

This book repeatedly stresses the importance of understanding the largest Materials firms given the sector's concentration (outlined in Chapter 4). For your reference, the following tables outline the largest Materials firms in the MSCI All Country World Index (ACWI) by industry as of December 31, 2007. The MSCI ACWI is one of the broadest indexes available—nearly all the world's largest Materials firms are included.

## Table B.1   Metals & Mining

| Company | Market Cap (Mil) | Country | Industry Weight (%) |
| --- | --- | --- | --- |
| BHP Billiton | $186,988 | Australia | 9.4 |
| Rio Tinto | $159,277 | UK | 8.0 |
| Cia Vale Do Rio Doce | $154,681 | Brazil | 7.8 |
| Arcelor-Mittal | $112,669 | France | 5.7 |
| Anglo American Plc | $81,060 | UK | 4.1 |
| Xstrata Plc | $68,664 | UK | 3.5 |
| Posco | $53,557 | South Korea | 2.7 |
| Norilsk Nickel | $50,516 | Russia | 2.5 |
| Nippon Steel Corp | $42,164 | Japan | 2.1 |
| Freeport-McMoran Copper & Gold | $39,124 | US | 2.0 |

*Source:* Thomson Datastream; MSCI, Inc.[1] as of 12/31/07.

## Table B.2    Chemicals

| Company | Market Cap (Mil) | Country | Industry Weight (%) |
| --- | --- | --- | --- |
| BASF Ag | $71,862 | Germany | 7.7 |
| Monsanto Co New | $61,073 | US | 6.6 |
| Potash Corp Of Saskatchewan | $45,966 | Canada | 4.9 |
| Mosaic Co | $41,682 | US | 4.5 |
| Du Pont (E.I.) De Nemours | $39,639 | US | 4.3 |
| Dow Chemical | $37,228 | US | 4.0 |
| Air Liquide | $35,540 | France | 3.8 |
| Praxair Inc | $28,024 | US | 3.0 |
| Shin-Etsu Chemical Co Ltd | $27,152 | Japan | 2.9 |
| Syngenta Ag | $25,676 | Switzerland | 2.8 |

*Source:* Thomson Datastream; MSCI, Inc.[2] as of 12/31/07.

## Table B.3    Construction Materials

| Company | Market Cap (Mil) | Country | Industry Weight (%) |
| --- | --- | --- | --- |
| Lafarge Sa | $31,723 | France | 12.6 |
| Holcim Ltd-Reg | $28,054 | Switzerland | 11.1 |
| Cemex Sa | $20,312 | Mexico | 8.1 |
| CRH Ord | $19,090 | Ireland | 7.6 |
| Heidelberger Zement Ag | $18,597 | Germany | 7.4 |
| Siam Cement Co. | $16,600 | Thailand | 6.6 |
| Grasim Industries Limited | $8,517 | India | 3.4 |
| Vulcan Materials Co | $7,560 | US | 3.0 |
| Cimpor-Cimentos De Portugal | $5,894 | Portugal | 2.3 |
| Ambuja Cements Limited | $5,677 | India | 2.3 |

*Source:* Thomson Datastream; MSCI, Inc.[3] as of 12/31/07.

## Table B.4    Paper & Forest Products

| Company | Market Cap (Mil) | Country | Industry Weight (%) |
|---------|------------------|---------|---------------------|
| Weyerhaeuser Co | $15,450 | US | 12.0 |
| International Paper Co | $13,863 | US | 10.7 |
| Nine Dragons Paper Holdings | $10,859 | China | 8.4 |
| Sca Sv Cellulosa B | $10,491 | Sweden | 8.1 |
| Upm-Kymmene Oyj | $10,356 | Finland | 8.0 |
| Stora Enso Oyj-R Shs | $9,163 | Finland | 7.1 |
| Empresas Cmpc Sa | $7,550 | Chile | 5.8 |
| Meadwestvaco Corp | $5,782 | US | 4.5 |
| Oji Paper Co Ltd | $5,230 | Japan | 4.0 |
| Lifestyle Intl Hldgs Ltd | $4,994 | Hong Kong | 3.9 |

*Source:* Thomson Datastream; MSCI, Inc.[4] as of 12/31/07.

## Table B.5    Containers & Packaging

| Company | Market Cap (Mil) | Country | Industry Weight (%) |
|---------|------------------|---------|---------------------|
| Owens-Illinois Inc | $7,760 | US | 15.6 |
| Rexam Plc | $5,351 | UK | 10.7 |
| Amcor Ltd | $5,269 | Australia | 10.6 |
| Ball Corp | $4,522 | US | 9.1 |
| Toyo Seikan Kaisha Ltd | $3,842 | Japan | 7.7 |
| Sealed Air Corp | $3,737 | US | 7.5 |
| Smurfit Kappa Group Plc | $3,567 | Ireland | 7.2 |
| Pactiv Corporation | $3,474 | US | 7.0 |
| Smurfit-Stone Container | $2,697 | US | 5.4 |
| Mayr-Melnhof Karton Ag | $2,384 | Austria | 4.8 |

*Source:* Thomson Datastream; MSCI, Inc.[5] as of 12/31/07.

# Notes

## CHAPTER 1: MATERIALS BASICS

1. Copyright © [2009] The McGraw-Hill Companies, Inc. Standard & Poor's, including its subsidiary corporations (S&P), is a division of the McGraw-Hill Companies, Inc. Reproduction of this work in any form is prohibited without S&P's prior written permission.
2. "Did you know?" European Copper Institute, http://www.eurocopper.org/copper/copper-usage.html (accessed July 14, 2008).
3. "Mineral Exploration and Mining," Satellite Imaging Corporation, http://www.satimagingcorp.com/svc/mining.html (accessed June 18, 2008).
4. "Exploration," *Engineering and Mining Journal* (April 2001).
5. Robert Guy Matthews, "Hunters Comb Globe for a Hot Metal," *Wall Street Journal* (April 4, 2008), http://online.wsj.com/article/SB120728123161288949.html?mod=hps_us_inside_today (accessed June 18, 2008).
6. Keith Campbell, "State Mining Royalties Proposals Improve, but Still Causing Some Concern," *Mining Weekly* (November 17, 2006), http://www.miningweekly.com/article.php?a_id=97472 (accessed August 14, 2008); International Finance Corporation Press Release, "IFC Helps Support Black Economic Empowerment in South Africa" (February 13, 2004), http://ifcln001.worldbank.org/ifcext/pressroom/ifcpressroom.nsf/PressRelease?openform&7BFB6F8A2076B59285256E3900546EBC (accessed July 29, 2008).
7. John D. Jorgenson, "2006 Minerals Yearbook: Iron Ore," U.S. Department of the Interior and U.S. Geological Survey (May 2008), http://minerals.usgs.gov/minerals/pubs/commodity/iron_ore/index.html (accessed July 14, 2008).
8. CEO of Titan International in Q4 2007 Earnings Call Transcript, page 9 of 15.
9. "Primary Copper Smelting," U.S. Environmental Protection Agency, http://www.epa.gov/ttn/chief/ap42/ch12/final/c12s03.pdf (accessed July 29, 2008).
10. Ibid.

11. Miho Yoshikawa, "Update 2- Japan, BHP Set 2008 Copper Fees at $45/4.5 Cents," *Reuters* (January 18, 2008), http://www.reuters.com/article/rbssIndustry-MaterialsUtilitiesNews/idUST3626520080118 (accessed July 29, 2008).

12. "Scrap Recycling Industry Facts," Institute of Scrap Recycling Industries, Inc., http://www.isri.org/AM/Template.cfm?Section=Home1&CONTENTID=160 96&TEMPLATE=/CM/ContentDisplay.cfm (accessed July 29, 2008).

13. See note 11.

14. British Cement Association, http://www.cementindustry.co.uk/.

15. "Cement & Concrete Basics," Portland Cement Association, http://www.cement.org/basics/concretebasics_concretebasics.asp (accessed July 29, 2008).

16. Ibid.

17. "How Portland Cement is Made," Portland Cement Association, http://www.cement.org/basics/howmade.asp (accessed July 30, 2008).

18. "Cement Industry Overview," Portland Cement Association, http://www.cement.org/econ/industry.asp (accessed July 7, 2008).

19. Ed Sullivan, "Capacity Expansion Update," *The Monitor,* Portland Cement Association (April 30, 2008), http://www.cement.org/econ/pdf/NONMEMBE RCapacityExpansion.pdf (accessed July 7, 2008).

20. "Coal and Cement," World Coal Institute, http://www.worldcoal.org/pages/content/index.asp?PageID=110 (accessed June 18, 2008).

21. Brian R. Hook, "Construction and Demolition Recycling Rates Climb," *American Recycler* (January 2007), http://www.americanrecycler.com/0107/construction.html (accessed August 14, 2008). Concrete Recycling Organization website presented by the Construction Materials Recycling Association, http://www.concreterecycling.org/ (accessed July 30, 2008).

22. "U.S. Hardwood Species," American Hardwood Export Council (2002), http://www.ahec.org/hardwoods/species.html (accessed July 30, 2008).

23. Neil K. Huyler and Chris B. LeDoux, "Performance of a Cut-to-Length Harvester in a Single-Tree and Group-Selection Cut," United States Department of Agriculture (November 1999), http://www.fs.fed.us/ne/newtown_square/pub-lications/research_papers/pdfs/scanned/OCR/ne_rp711.pdf (accessed June 18, 2008).

24. "Paper Production and Consumption Facts," Co-op America, http://www.coo-pamerica.org/programs/woodwise/consumers/stats/index.cfm (accessed July 30, 2008).

25. See note 11.

26. "Collection: Recycling in the Paper Industry," Institute of Paper Science and Technology at Georgia Tech (June 13, 2006), http://www.ipst.gatech.edu/amp/collection/museum_recycling.htm (accessed June 18, 2008).

27. "Facts about Paper Recycling," American Forest & Paper Association, http://www.afandpa.org/Content/NavigationMenu/Environment_and_Recycling/Recycling/Facts_About_Paper_Recycling/Facts_About_Paper_Recycling.htm (accessed July 30, 2008).

## CHAPTER 2: A BRIEF HISTORY OF MATERIALS

1. "Industry Comes of Age: 1865–1900," http://www.course-notes.org/us_history/american_pageant_11th_edition_outlines/chapter_25_-_industry_comes_of_age/ (accessed July 2, 2008).

2. Carolyn Dimitri, Anne Effland, and Neilson Conklin, "The 20th Century Transformation of U.S. Agriculture and Farm Policy," U.S. Department of Agriculture (June 2005), http://www.ers.usda.gov/publications/EIB3/EIB3.htm (accessed July 2, 2008).

3. Yves Meny, Vincent Wright, and Martin Rhodes, *The Politics of Steel: Western Europe and the Steel Industry in the Crisis Years (1974–1984)* (New York: Walter De Gruyter, 1987).

4. American Society of Civil Engineers, "An Action Plan For the 110th Congress," Report Card for America's Infrastructure (2008), http://www.asce.org/report-card/2005/actionplan07.cfm (accessed June 18, 2008).

## CHAPTER 3: MATERIALS SECTOR DRIVERS

1. Michael George, "2006 Minerals Yearbook: Platinum-Group Metals," U.S. Department of the Interior and U.S. Geological Survey (September 2007), http://minerals.usgs.gov/minerals/pubs/commodity/platinum/ (accessed July 1, 2008).

2. John D. Jorgenson, "2006 Minerals Yearbook: Iron Ore," U.S. Department of the Interior and U.S. Geological Survey (May 2008), http://minerals.usgs.gov/minerals/pubs/commodity/iron_ore/index.html (accessed July 10, 2008). Page 39.4; BHP Billiton, February 6th, 2008 interim presentation.

3. "Platinum," New York Mercantile Exchange (2006), http://www.nymex.com/pla_fut_descri.aspx (accessed July 10, 2008).

4. "S. African Power Crisis: Eskom's Generating Capacity," *Reuters Africa* (March 18, 2008), http://africa.reuters.com/energyandoil/news/usnL18624120.html (accessed July 10, 2008).

5. Thomson Financial, "Rio Tinto Secures 85 Percent Rise in 2008 Iron Ore Contract Prices," *Forbes* (June 23, 2008), http://global.forbes.com/feeds/afx/2008/06/23/afx5143385.html (accessed July 17, 2008). United Steelworkers, "Australian Rain Plus Chinese Demand Equals Higher Coal Prices," (June 5,

2008), http://www.uswa.ca/program/printthispage.php?pageid=5072&lan=en (accessed July 17, 2008).

6. Daniel L. Edelstein, "2006 Minerals Yearbook: Copper," U.S. Department of Interior and U.S. Geological Survey (May 2008), http://minerals.usgs.gov/minerals/pubs/commodity/copper/ (accessed July 14, 2008).

7. Ibid.

8. London Metal Exchange, http://www.lme/co.uk.

9. BHP Billiton February 6th, 2008 interim presentation.

10. See note 11.

11. Thompson Street Events, February 2008 Morgan Stanley Basic Materials Conference, Page 1.

12. Thompson Street Events, Freeport Mcmoran Q4 2007, conference call.

## CHAPTER 4: MATERIALS SECTOR BREAKDOWN

1. Source: MSCI. The MSCI information may only be used for your internal use, may not be reproduced or redisseminated in any form, and may not be used to create any financial instruments or products or any indices. The MSCI information is provided on an "as is" basis and the user of this information assumes the entire risk of any use made of this information. MSCI, each of its affiliates, and each other person involved in or related to compiling, computing, or creating any MSCI information (collectively, the "MSCI Parties") expressly disclaims all warranties (including, without limitation, any warranties of originality, accuracy, completeness, timeliness, non-infringement, merchantability, and fitness for a particular purpose) with respect to this information. Without limiting any of the foregoing, in no event shall any MSCI Party have any liability for any direct, indirect, special, incidental, punitive, consequential (including, without limitation, lost profits), or any other damages.

2. Ibid.

3. Ibid.

4. Ibid.

5. Ibid.

6. Ibid.

7. Ibid.

8. "Mine—As Good as it Gets?" PriceWaterhouseCoopers (2008), http://www.pwc.com/extweb/pwcpublications.nsf/docid/4E436FE336691 8688525746B005C8D9E/$File/Mine_2008_v7_Final.pdf (accessed August 6, 2008).

9. John D. Jorgenson, "2006 Minerals Yearbook: Iron Ore," U.S. Department of the Interior and U.S. Geological Survey (May 2008), http://minerals.

usgs.gov/minerals/pubs/commodity/iron_ore/index.html (accessed July 14, 2008).

10. Ibid. The Empire State Building facts from The New York-Travel Information Center, http://www.newyorktransportation.com/info/empirefact2.html.

11. Michael D. Fenton, "2006 Minerals Yearbook: Iron and Steel," U.S. Department of Interior and U.S. Geological Survey, http://minerals.usgs.gov/minerals/pubs/commodity/iron_&_steel/myb1-2006-feste.pdf (accessed July 14, 2008).

12. "The World's Top Ten Corporate Iron Ore Producers," *Reuters* (October 22, 2007), http://uk.reuters.com/article/oilRpt/idUKSP7026220071022 (accessed July 16, 2008); "Iron Ore Producers," EconStats, http://www.econstats.com/rt_ironore.htm (accessed July 16, 2008).

13. International Iron and Steel Institute, "Crude Steel Production by Process, 2006," http://www.worldsteel.org/?action=storypages&id=196 (accessed July 16, 2008).

14. "International Energy Outlook 2007," US Department of Energy, Energy Information Administration (May 2007), http://www.eia.doe.gov/oiaf/ieo/coal.html (accessed May 8, 2008).

15. "Coal Market & Pricing," World Coal Institute, http://www.worldcoal.org/pages/content/index.asp?PageID=438 (accessed August 6, 2008).

16. 2007 BP Statistical Review of World Energy, http://www.bp.com.

17. "Top Steel-Producing Companies, 2005 and 2006," International Iron and Steel Institute, http://www.worldsteel.org/?action=storypages&id=194 (accessed July 16, 2008).

18. David Phelps, "Outlook for the U.S. Steel Market in 2008 Presentation," American Institute for International Steel (February 19, 2008), http://www.aiis.org/index.php?tg=articles&idx=Print&topics=20&article=301 (accessed July 17, 2008).

19. "AISI Market Development Progress Report 2006–2007," American Iron and Steel Institute, http://www.steel.org/AM/Template.cfm?Section=Annual_Reports1&CONTENTID=20664&TEMPLATE=/CM/ContentDisplay.cfm (accessed July 16, 2008).

20. See note 13.

21. "Gold Demand Trends: Full year and Fourth Quarter 2007," World Gold Council (February 2008), http://www.gold.org/deliver.php?file=/assets/file/pub_archive/pdf/GDT_Q4_2007.pdf (accessed August 6, 2008).

22. Goldsheet Mining Directory, World Gold Production (http://www.goldsheetlinks.com/production.htm).

23. Claudia Carpenter, "Copper Climbs After Stockpiles Decline; Aluminum Erases Advance," Bloomberg (June 27, 2008), http://www.bloomberg.com/apps/news?pid=20601012&sid=aVj3KzKPKHbQ&refer=commodities (accessed August 13, 2008).

24. The Aluminum Association, http://www.aluminum.org/AM/Template.cfm?S ection=Overview&Template=/CM/HTMLDisplay.cfm&ContentID=26509 (accessed July 17, 2008).

25. "Global Ethylene and Propylene Demand and Capacity to See a Dramatic Change," Plastemart, http://www.plastemart.com/upload/Literature/Global-ethylene-propylene-demand-capacity-to-change.asp (accessed August 13, 2008).

26. Doug Smock, "Boeing 787 Dreamliner Represents Composites Revolution," *Design News* (June 4, 2007), http://www.designnews.com/index.asp?layout=art icle&articleid=CA6441583 (accessed June 24, 2008); Ed Grabianowski, "How the Airbus A380 Works," How Stuff Works, http://travel.howstuffworks.com/ a380.htm/printable (accessed June 24, 2008).

27. Ben Rasmussen, "Market Trends: This Industry is Ready to Explode," Zoltek (March 27, 2008), http://www.zoltek.com/aboutus/news/91/ (accessed August 13, 2008).

28. "The Global Benefits of Eating Less Meat," Compassion in World Farming Trust, (2004), p. 7, http://209.85.173.104/search?q=cache:LsXongIafToJ:www.ciwf. org/publications/reports/The_Global_Benefits_of_Eating_Less_Meat.pdf+pound s+of+grain+per+meat&hl=en&ct=clnk&cd=7&gl=us (accessed June 24, 2008).

29. "Staying Home: How Ethanol Will Change U.S. Corn Exports," The Institute for Agriculture and Trade Policy, http://www.agobservatory.org/library. cfm?refid=96658 (accessed June 25, 2008).

30. Paul C. Westcott, "U.S. Ethanol Expansion Driving Changes Throughout the Agricultural Sector," United States Department of Agriculture (September 2007), http://www.ers.usda.gov/AmberWaves/September07/Features/Ethanol. htm (accessed June 25, 2008); Ephraim Leibtag, "Corn Prices Near Record High, But What About Food Costs?" United States Department of Agriculture (February 2008), http://www.ers.usda.gov/AmberWaves/February08/Features/ CornPrices.htm (accessed June 25, 2008); "Agrium: Transformation & Growth" (February 2008), http://www.agrium.com/uploads/Morgan_Stanley_08.pdf (accessed June 25, 2008).

31. "Global Environment Outlook," United Nations Environment Programme (2007), p. 110, http://www.unep.org/geo/geo4/report/GEO-4_Report_Full_ en.pdf (accessed June 24, 2008).

32. Anand Giridharadas, "In India, Mom and Pop Get Shoved Aside," *International Herald Tribune* (October 24, 2006), http://www.iht.com/articles/2006/10/19/ business/retail.php (accessed June 25, 2008).

33. "Biotech Crops Experience Remarkable Dozen Years of Double-Digit Growth," International Service for the Acquisition of Agri-Biotech Applications, ISAAA Brief 37-2007 Press Release(February 13, 2008), http://www.isaaa.org/resources/ publications/briefs/37/pressrelease/default.html (accessed June 25, 2008).

34. K.S. Jayaraman, "India Approves Cultivation of GM Crops," Science and Development Network (March 26, 2002), http://www.scidev.net/en/news/india-approves-cultivation-of-gm-crops.html (accessed June 25, 2008); Don Ethridge, "Changes in Global Cotton Markets: Causes and Effects," Cotton Economics Research Institute, Texas Tech University (September 11, 2007), http://www.aaec.ttu.edu/CERI/policy/includes/WCRC4%20Presentation%20(2).ppt?bcsi_scan_34E336E4D93AA9DD=0&bcsi_scan_filename=WCRC4%20Presentation%20(2).ppt#260,5,Slide%205 (accessed June 25, 2008).

35. Mica Rosenberg, "Mexico Approves Rules To Begin Planting GM Corn," Planet Ark (March 25, 2008), http://www.planetark.org/dailynewsstory.cfm/newsid/47627/story.htm (accessed June 25, 2008).

36. "Whole Farm Nutrient Management Tutorials," Cornell University, http://instruct1.cit.cornell.edu/Courses/css412/mod3/ext_m3_pg6.htm (accessed June 25, 2008).

37. International Fertilizer Industry Association, http://www.fertilizer.org/ifa/Home-Page/STATISTICS/Production-and-trade-statistics (accessed August 15, 2008).

38. Industrial Gas Plants, http://www.industrialgasplants.com/industry-overview.html (accessed August 13, 2008).

39. "Overview of the Cement Industry," Portland Cement Association (May 2003), http://www.cement.org/basics/cementindustry.asp (accessed June 25, 2008).

40. See note 1.

41. "Wood for Paper: Fiber Sourcing in the Global Pulp and Paper Industry," Seneca Creek Associates, LLC and Wood Resources International, LLC, (December 2007), http://www.afandpa.org/temp/AFPAFiberSourcingPape12-07.pdf?bcsi_scan_408DE456E3075246=1 (accessed July 9, 2008).

42. Co-op America, Paper Production and Consumption Facts, http://www.coopamerica.org/programs/woodwise/consumers/stats/index.cfm (accessed August 13, 2008).

43. See note 41.

44. Daniel Dufour, "The Lumber Industry: Crucial Contribution to Canada's Prosperity," Statistics Canada, http://dsp-psd.tpsgc.gc.ca/Collection/Statcan/31F0027M/31F0027MIE2002001.pdf (accessed August 13, 2008).

45. Ibid.

46. Kathie Durban, "Spotted Owl or Red Herring?" *High Country News* (March 20, 2006), http://www.hcn.org/servlets/hcn.Article?article_id=16177 (accessed August 13, 2008).

47. "Issues: Wildlands," National Resources Defense Council (February 19, 2008), http://www.nrdc.org/land/forests/qroadless.asp (accessed June 25, 2008).

48. World Forest Institute, http://wfi.worldforestrycenter.org/trade-3.htm (accessed August 13, 2008).
49. Packaging Today, http://www.packagingtoday.com/packagingindustrymergers.html (accessed August 13, 2008).

## CHAPTER 5: STAYING CURRENT: TRACKING SECTOR FUNDAMENTALS

1. "Production and International Trade Statistics," International Fertilizer Industry Association (September 27, 2007), http://www.fertilizer.org/ifa/statistics/pit_public/pit_public_statistics.asp (accessed July 21, 2008).

## CHAPTER 6: CASE STUDY: THE 2003 TO 2007 BULL MARKET IN MATERIALS

1. 2006 Iron Ore Minerals Yearbook; The World Copper Factbook 2007.
2. Global Financial Data, https://globalfinancialdata.com.
3. "Global Infrastructure Spending to Rise," KHL's World Construction Week (January 17, 2007), http://crgp.stanford.edu/news/global_projects_realnews_global_infrastructure_spending_to_rise.html (accessed June 23, 2008); Graham Summers, "$300 Billion Explosion in the Middle East," The Growth Stock Wire (April 20, 2007), http://www.growthstockwire.com/archive/2007/apr/2007_apr_20.asp (accessed June 23, 2008).
4. Richard R. Wertz, "Three Gorges Dam," http://www.ibiblio.org/chinesehistory/contents/07spe/specrep01.html (accessed August 15, 2008); "Great Wall Across the Yangtze," http://www.pbs.org/itvs/greatwall/ (accessed June 23, 2008).
5. James Russell, "Coal Use Rises Dramatically Despite Impacts on Climate and Health," Worldwatch Institute (2008), http://www.worldwatch.org/node/5508 (accessed June 20, 2008). DUPE.
6. BP Statistical Review of World Energy, Coal Consumption Table, June 2008, http://www.bp.com/sectiongenericarticle.do?categoryId=9023786&contentId=7044482 (accessed August 15, 2008).
7. Aggregate & Ready Mix Association of Minnesota, http://www.armofmn.com/resources/aggregates.html.
8. Calum MacLeod, "China's Highways Go the Distance," USA Today (January 29, 2006), http://www.usatoday.com/news/world/2006-01-29-china-roads_x.htm (accessed June 23, 2008). DUPE; Robert E. Skinner Jr., "Highway Design and Construction: The Innovation Challenge," National Academy of Engineering (Summer 2008), http://www.nae.edu/nae/bridgecom.nsf/weblinks/MKEZ-7FPKMW?OpenDocument (accessed August 15, 2008).

9. "World Crude Steel Production, 1950 to 2006," International Iron and Steel Institute, http://www.worldsteel.org/?action=storypages&id=193 (accessed July 16, 2008); Metal Producing & Processing Staff, "Global Steel Output Rose 7.5% in 2007," *Metal Producing & Processing* (January 24, 2008), http://www.metal-producing.com/redirect/feature/79229/global_steel_output_rose_75_in_2007 (accessed July 16, 2008).

10. "Apparent Steel Use, 2000 to 2006," International Iron and Steel Institute, http://www.worldsteel.org/?action=storypages&id=205 (accessed July 16, 2008).

11. Cleveland-Cliffs B of A Presentation (May 7, 2008), http://www.b2i.us/profiles/investor/fullpage.asp?f=1&BzID=1041&to=cp&Nav=0&LangID=1&s=0&ID=2228 (accessed July 16, 2008). DUPE.

12. "Major Steel-Producing Countries, 2005 and 2006," International Iron and Steel Institute, http://www.worldsteel.org/?action=storypages&id=195 (accessed July 17, 2008).

13. BHP Billiton February 6th, 2008 interim presentation, page 18; Vale Q2 2008 Earnings Presentation, page 11.

14. BHP Billiton February 6th, 2008 interim presentation, page 18.

15. Vale Q2 2008 Earnings Presentation, page 11; "China's Copper and Aluminum Consumption for Jan–Mar 2008," World Aluminum Market (May 16, 2008), http://www.world-aluminium-market.com/market/stat/others/consumption/ (accessed July 17, 2008).

16. "World Urbanization Prospects: The 2007 Revision," Department of Economic and Social Affairs (February 2008), http://www.un.org/esa/population/publications/wup2007/2007WUP_Highlights_web.pdf (accessed June 19, 2008). DUPE.

17. Ibid.

18. Ibid.

19. Rita Raagas De Ramos, "Infrastructure Spending to Surge in Emerging Markets," *BusinessWeek* (June 25, 2008), http://www.businessweek.com/globalbiz/content/jun2008/gb20080625_321091.htm?chan=top+news_top+news+index_global+business (accessed July 11, 2008).

20. "Infrastructure and the World Bank: A Progress Report," Development Committee World Bank (September 6, 2005), http://siteresources.worldbank.org/DEVCOMMINT/Documentation/20651863/DC2005-0015(E)-Infrastructure.pdf (accessed June 19, 2008).

21. Rio Tinto Investor Presentation, Australian Site Visit, June 15, 2008.

22. "U.S. Auto Sales Will Rebound in 2009 as Opportunities in Developing Countries Grow; OEMs, Suppliers Must Carefully Consider Unique Aspects of Each Market," CSM Worldwide (April 3, 2008), http://www.csmauto.com/

news/in-the-press/2008/04/03/131 (accessed June 19, 2008); "CSM Global Production Summary by Region & Country," CSM Worldwide, http://www.automotiveforecasting.com/gpo/Global-Summary-by-Country.pdf (accessed June 19, 2008).

23. Lester R. Brown, Michael Renner, and Christopher Flavin, *Vital Signs 1998: The Environmental Trends That Are Shaping Our Future* (W.W. Norton & Company, 1998).

24. "Report Card for America's Infrastructure," American Society of Civil Engineers, http://www.asce.org/files/pdf/reportcard/2005_Report_Card-Full_Report.pdf (accessed June 23, 2008). DUPE.

25. Stephen Flynn, "Minn. Bridge Collapse Reveals Brittle America: Expert Op-Ed," *Popular Mechanics* (August 2, 2007), http://www.popularmechanics.com/technology/transportation/4219981.html (accessed June 23, 2008); "$38 Million Deal Reached in Minn. Bridge Collapse," *CNN* (May 2, 2008), http://www.cnn.com/2008/US/05/02/bridge.collapse/?iref=mpstoryview (accessed June 23, 2008).

26. James Barron, "Steam Blast Jolts Midtown, Killing One," *New York Times* (July 19, 2007), http://www.nytimes.com/2007/07/19/nyregion/19explode.html?hp (accessed June 23, 2008).

27. Report Card for America's Infrastructure, "National Fact Sheet," American Society of Civil Engineers, http://www.asce.org/reportcard/2005/page.cfm?id=145 (accessed June 23, 2008). DUPE.

28. The White House, "President Signs Transportation Act," Office of the Press Secretary (August 10, 2005), http://www.whitehouse.gov/news/releases/2005/08/20050810-1.html (accessed June 24, 2008); California State Auditor, "The California State Auditor's Initial Assessment of High-Risk Issues the State and Select State Agencies Face," Bureau of State Audits (May 2007), http://www.bsa.ca.gov/reports/summary.php?id=535 (accessed June 24, 2008).

29. Thompson Street Event, Q4 2006 transcript. Page 4.

30. Caterpillar Mining Truck specifications, http://www.teknoxgroup.com/images/specalogs/eng/797B.pdf?bcsi_scan_34E336E4D93AA9DD=pMPZO579mfp2B0eYp2gASAIAAACs2YQA:1 (accessed June 25, 2008); Simon Romero, "Big Tires in Short Supply," *New York Times* (April 20, 2006), http://www.nytimes.com/2006/04/20/business/20tire.html?_r=1&oref=slogin (accessed June 25, 2008).

31. Matthew Warren, "Coal Ship Queue to Last for Months," *The Australian* (March 27, 2007), http://www.theaustralian.news.com.au/story/0,25197,21452339-2702,00.html (accessed June 25, 2008).

32. Scott Wright, "Gold Mining Challenges," Zeal Speculation and Investment (September 28, 2007), http://www.zealllc.com/2007/goldmine.htm (accessed

June 25, 2008); "Venezuela Nationalizes Steel Industry," *CNN* (May 1, 2008), http://edition.cnn.com/2008/WORLD/americas/05/01/venezuela.steel/index. html (accessed June 25, 2008).

33. Milagros Salazar, "Peru: 'Voluntary Payment' Instead of Taxes for Mining Firms," CorpWatch (August 25, 2006), http://www.corpwatch.org/article. php?id=14069 (accessed June 25, 2008).

34. Nathan Becker, "Fraser Survey Shows Big Dips in Chile, Mongolia for Mining," *Resource Investor* (March 5, 2007), http://www.resourceinvestor.com/ pebble.asp?relid=29541 (accessed June 25, 2008).

35. Ginger Ding, "Indian Iron Ore Export Tax May Deter China," *Resource Investor* (January 15, 2008), http://www.resourceinvestor.com/pebble.asp?relid=39506 (accessed June 25, 2008).

36. Bloomberg Finance L.P., http://www.bloomberg.com.

37. Donald Greenlees, "Indonesian Court Acquits Newmont Mining," *New York Times* (April 25, 2007), http://www.nytimes.com/2007/04/25/world/asia/ 25indo.html?pagewanted=1 (accessed June 25, 2008).

38. Thomson Reuters; as of 12/31/07, deal value and volume represent public and private deals.

## CHAPTER 7: THE TOP-DOWN METHOD

1. Matthew Kalman, "Einstein Letters Reveal a Turmoil Beyond Science," *Boston Globe* (July 11, 2006), http://www.boston.com/news/world/middleeast/arti- cles/2006/07/11/einstein_letters_reveal_a_turmoil_beyond_science/ (accessed May 9, 2008).

2. Berkshire Hathaway 2005 Annual Report.

3. Michael Michalko, "Combinatory Play," Creative Thinking, http://www .creativethinking.net/DT10_CombinatoryPlay.htm?Entry=Good (accessed May 9, 2008).

4. Gary P. Brinson, Brian D. Singer, and Gilbert L. Beebower, "Determinants of Portfolio Performance II: An Update," *The Financial Analysts Journal* 47 (1991 [3]): 40–48.

5. Source: MSCI. The MSCI information may only be used for your internal use, may not be reproduced or redisseminated in any form and may not be used to create any financial instruments or products or any indices. The MSCI information is provided on an "as is" basis and the user of this information assumes the entire risk of any use made of this information. MSCI, each of its affiliates and each other person involved in or related to compiling, computing, or creating any MSCI information (collectively, the "MSCI Parties") expressly disclaims all warranties (including, without limitation, any warranties of origi- nality, accuracy, completeness, timeliness, non-infringement, merchantability,

and fitness for a particular purpose) with respect to this information. Without limiting any of the foregoing, in no event shall any MSCI Party have any liability for any direct, indirect, special, incidental, punitive, consequential (including, without limitation, lost profits), or any other damages.

6. Ibid.
7. Ibid.
8. Ibid.
9. Ibid.
10. Ibid.

## CHAPTER 9: MATERIALIZE YOUR PORTFOLIO: INVESTING STRATEGIES

1. Source: MSCI. The MSCI information may only be used for your internal use, may not be reproduced or redisseminated in any form and may not be used to create any financial instruments or products or any indices. The MSCI information is provided on an "as is" basis and the user of this information assumes the entire risk of any use made of this information. MSCI, each of its affiliates, and each other person involved in or related to compiling, computing, or creating any MSCI information (collectively, the "MSCI Parties") expressly disclaims all warranties (including, without limitation, any warranties of originality, accuracy, completeness, timeliness, non-infringement, merchantability, and fitness for a particular purpose) with respect to this information. Without limiting any of the foregoing, in no event shall any MSCI Party have any liability for any direct, indirect, special, incidental, punitive, consequential (including, without limitation, lost profits), or any other damages.

## APPENDIX B

1. Source: MSCI. The MSCI information may only be used for your internal use, may not be reproduced or redisseminated in any form and may not be used to create any financial instruments or products or any indices. The MSCI information is provided on an "as is" basis and the user of this information assumes the entire risk of any use made of this information. MSCI, each of its affiliates, and each other person involved in or related to compiling, computing, or creating any MSCI information (collectively, the "MSCI Parties") expressly disclaims all warranties (including, without limitation, any warranties of originality, accuracy, completeness, timeliness, non-infringement, merchantability, and fitness

for a particular purpose) with respect to this information. Without limiting any of the foregoing, in no event shall any MSCI Party have any liability for any direct, indirect, special, incidental, punitive, consequential (including, without limitation, lost profits), or any other damages.

2. Ibid.
3. Ibid.
4. Ibid.
5. Ibid.

# Glossary

**Aluminum**　A metal often used to form light, corrosion-resistant alloys. Aluminum is the most abundant metallic ore in the earth's crust.

**Ammonia**　A colorless gas that is often used to manufacture fertilizers and a wide variety of nitrogen-based chemicals.

**Anode**　The fourth stage of metal smelting. Anodes are typically 99 percent pure metal. Metals of this quality are used for many purposes in construction.

**Backwardation**　A situation in which the future price of a commodity is lower than the current price of commodity; the opposite of contango.

**Baltic Dry Index**　An index created by the London-based Baltic Exchange that measures changes in the cost to transport raw materials such as metals and grains by sea.

**Bar Steel**　Usually formed from carbon steel, bar steel is commonly used in reinforced concrete and reinforced masonry structures. It is often given ridges for better frictional adhesion to the concrete.

**Barrier to Entry**　Obstacles such as high costs or regulatory hurdles that prevent new competitors from easily entering a business or industry.

**Base Metal**　Non-ferrous metal, excluding precious metals.

**Basic Oxygen Furnace (BOF)**　A furnace used in the steelmaking process to convert the molten iron from a blast furnace into refined steel.

**Blister**　The result of the third stage in metal smelting. It typically has a 95 to 98 percent metal concentration. It is named "Blister" due to the blisters that form on the metal as the result of having hot air blown through it as part of the refining process.

**Capacity Utilization Rate**    A metric, generally expressed as a percentage, which is used to measure the extent to which a company is maximizing output. Generally, high capacity utilization rates tend to be indicative of tight market fundamentals for the product being produced.

**Capital Intensive**    A business process or an industry that requires a significant amount of capital relative to labor to produce a given good. It is often characteristic of businesses with high fixed investment costs. Capital intensive industries tend to have higher barriers to entry due to the high level of initial investment that is required.

**Cathode**    The fifth and last stage of metal refining. Cathodes are typically 99.99 percent pure metal. Only metals that require the highest degree of purity are turned into cathodes. One example is copper wiring. Pure copper is a more efficient conductor of electricity.

**Cement Clinker**    Cement clinkers are formed during the processing of cement in a kiln. Limestone, clay, and other ingredients are heated in specific proportions in a rotating kiln until they begin to form cement clinkers. Cement clinkers are usually ground with gypsum to produce the fine powder later mixed with liquid to produce cement.

**Cold-Rolled Coil Steel**    Flat rolled products that are rolled in a Cold Strip Mill at room temperature. The advantages of cold-rolled strip over hot strip lie in better surface quality and thinner sections.

**Concentrate**    In the metals and mining industry, concentrate generally refers to metallic ore with about a 15 to 35 percent metal concentration. It is the result of the first stage in processing after mining and must be smelted to become refined metal.

**Concrete**    A construction material consisting of cement, as well as other materials such as construction aggregate.

**Construction Aggregate**    Material used in construction, generally in conjunction with cement. Aggregate may include sand, gravel, crushed stone, slag, and recycled concrete.

**Contango**    A situation in which the price of a commodity for future deliver is higher than the current price of the commodity; the opposite of backwardation.

**Cost Curve**    Within the Metals & Mining industry, it is a graphical representation of the cost of production for all producers of a given metal. It is most often graphed by producer, region, and individual mine.

**Downstream**    A relative term referring to the latter stages of the production process. For example, steelmaking might be said to be "downstream" to iron ore mining, as steelmakers use iron to create a value-added production.

**Durable Good**   A category of goods designed to last over three years. Automobiles and airplanes are examples of durable goods.

**Electric Arc Furnace (EAF)**   A furnace used in the steelmaking process that re-melts steel scrap into usable steel products. Electric Arc Furnaces are also known as "mini-mills."

**Ethylene**   Ethylene is produced from hydrocarbons in a process called steam cracking. Ethylene is primarily produced as a building block for other industrial chemicals. It is one of the simplest hydrocarbons and heavily used as a building block for more complex chemicals.

**Fixed Cost**   A cost that remains constant, regardless of the level of quantity of goods produced. Capital intensive businesses generally have a higher proportion of fixed costs.

**Flat Steel**   Steel that is rolled from carbon steel slabs into flat sections.

**Force Majeure**   French for "greater force," this is often a clause included in contracts designed to free parties from liability or obligation when a circumstance beyond their control prevents them from fulfilling their contractual obligations.

**Fungible**   A good is said to be fungible if any one unit can be equally exchanged for another unit. For example, copper might be said to be fungible because one ton of copper is substantially equal to another ton of copper.

**Futures Curve**   The set of prices at a given date for futures contracts on a given asset with different settlement dates. It is differentiated from a forward curve by the underlying asset, which must be traded on futures exchange.

**Futures Exchange**   A marketplace for the exchange of futures. Futures are a standardized contract to buy or sell a certain underlying good (e.g., a metal) at a given future date at a specified future price.

**Galvanized Steel**   Flat carbon steel products coated with zinc in order to provide corrosion protection.

**Genetically Modified**   An organism (typically an agricultural production) that has had its characteristics modified by the alteration or insertion of a gene.

**Hardwood**   The wood of a dicotyledonous tree, which produces seeds with a covering such as fruits and nuts. Typically of greater density, durability, and higher value than softwood. Often used in furniture and flooring.

**Hot-Rolled Coil Steel**   A steel product that is rolled through a Hot Strip Mill at high temperatures.

**Industrialization**   A process of economic development in which a society is transformed into an economy based on industry rather than agriculture. It is generally part of a broader modernization process that often involves the acceleration of large-scale energy and metallurgy production.

**Iron Ore Fines**   Fine grain-sized pieces of iron ore and smaller. It has the lowest value of three types of iron ore due to its small size, which makes it the least efficient for steelmaking due to the dust escaping in steam and smoke.

**Iron Ore Lumps**   Iron ore produced as lumps, often as large as a golf ball. Lumps come from the same mines and are made of the same material as fines, but are larger and therefore more efficient in the steelmaking process.

**Iron Ore Pellets**   Semi-processed iron clumped together in pellets with clay. Iron ore pellets tend to have a higher iron content than iron ore fines or iron ore lumps.

**Lignin**   The chemical compound that works as a natural glue to hold cellulose fibers together in wood.

**Marginal Cost of Production**   The change in total cost that arises when the quantity produced changes by one unit; the marginal cost is the cost of the next unit produced.

**Matte**   The result of the second stage in metal smelting. Matte typically has a 40 to 60 percent metal concentration.

**Metallurgical Coal**   A fine coal that is ground into powder and heated in coke ovens to produce coke. Coke is used as an agent in the blast-furnace production of iron.

**Metric Ton (Tonne)**   A unit of weight equivalent to 1,000 kilograms (or 2,204 pounds).

**Mineral Rights**   The right to extract a mineral from the earth, usually received in exchange for a royalty on sales of the mineral.

**Mini-mill**   A type of steel mill that uses Electric Arc Furnaces to re-melt scrap into usable steel. It is often located regionally and is able to start and stop production more efficiently than a traditional steel mill using iron ore-based blast furnaces.

**Non-Residential Construction**   The construction of any permanent structure not used for residential purposes. This includes both public infrastructure and commercial development.

**Open Pit Mine**   An aptly named method of mining in which ore and waste are extracted from the surface of the ground, often resulting in a large pit.

**Phosphate**   A phosphorus-based chemical that is mined from the ground and often used for agricultural fertilizer.

**Pig Iron**   A ferrous product produced by smelting iron ore with coke. Pig iron is often used in basic oxygen furnaces to produce steel.

**Pig Iron Nickel**   Also referred to as nickel chromium pig iron, pig iron nickel is an iron and nickel alloy used as a precursor for stainless steel and produced from low grade nickel laterite ore, which is primarily found in Indonesia and the Philippines.

**Price Cap**   The maximum rate or price, usually determined by a government organization, which can be charged for a particular good or service.

**Price Elasticity**   A measure of the responsiveness of the quantity of a good demanded due to a change in its price. A product with a high price elasticity of demand would show a large change in quantity demanded relative to a change in price.

**Potash**   Potassium or a potassium compound, often used as fertilizer in the agricultural industry.

**Propylene**   Similar to Ethylene. Propylene is produced from hydrocarbons in a process called steam cracking. Propylene is used as a raw material for the production of industrial chemicals. It is one of the simplest hydrocarbons and heavily used as a building block for more complex chemicals.

**Residential Construction**   The construction of a single-family home or townhouse. A form of private fixed-investment.

**Sawmill**   A mill or machine for sawing logs into lumber.

**Scrap Metal**   Discarded metal waste material that can be recycled in non-ferrous metal smelters or steel mills.

**Short Ton (Ton)**   2,000 pounds. A ton, as commonly used in the US and Canada.

**Slag**   The ferrous residue resulting from the smelting of iron ore with coking coal.

**Smelter**   A processing plant used to extract and refine metal from unrefined ore. It plays a similar role in metal refining as an oil refinery does in oil refining. Different metals often require different smelting processes.

**Softwood**   The wood of a coniferous tree, which produces seeds without a covering. Softwood tends to be softer and less dense than hardwood. It is primarily used in residential construction.

**Stainless Steel**   Steel that has been alloyed with at least 10 percent chromium, and often containing other elements (such as nickel) that are resistant to corrosion or rusting.

**Steam Coal**   Coal used in power plant and industrial steam boilers to produce electricity.

**Steel**   A durable metal alloyed from iron and carbon and widely used as a structural material.

**Steel Service Center**   A distribution center that purchases primary steel products from mills. It also often fabricates the steel to the end user's specification.

**Tariff**   Taxes imposed on the import or export of goods or services.

**Treatment and Refinement Charge (TC/RC)**   Fees smelters charge to form a metal into an anode (treatment charge) and to refine it into a cathode (refinement charge).

**Upstream**   A relative term referring to earlier stages in the production process, close to the start or source of production. For example, iron ore mining might be said to be "upstream" to steelmaking, as iron ore is necessary for steel production.

**Urea**   A nitrogen-based substance that is widely used in the agricultural industry as a fertilizer.

**Value-to-weight ratio**   A metric generally used to evaluate the commerciality of transporting a good. If a good has a low value-to-weight ratio, the revenues from the sale of the good may not be sufficient to offset the cost of transporting it.

**Variable Costs**   Expenses that change in portion to the quantity of goods or services produced.

**Vertical Integration**   When a company operates in the upstream and downstream stages of a production process, they are said to be vertically integrated.

**Windfall Tax**   A type of tax that governments often levy on resource industries when economic conditions allow them to attain above-average profits.

# About the Authors

**Brad W. Pyles** (San Francisco, California) is a capital markets analyst at Fisher Investments with a focus on Materials and macroeconomic strategy. He regularly presents to audiences at investing seminars and educational workshops across the country. He graduated from UCLA with a BA in Business Economics and a minor in Mathematics. Originally from Honolulu, he now resides in San Francisco with his wife, Tina.

**Andrew S. Teufel** (San Francisco, California) has been a member of Fisher Investments research staff since 1995 and is currently Co-President and Director of Research. Prior to joining the firm, he worked at Bear Stearns as a corporate finance analyst. He is a graduate of the University of California at Berkeley, and has lectured at the Haas School of Business on topics in investment management. Andrew has conducted hundreds of investment seminars and educational workshops throughout the US and the UK. He also serves as Editor-in-Chief of MarketMinder.com.

# Index